www.tredition.de

AF177112

Egon Harings

Germany after World War II

Two German states and their reunification

© 2018 Egon Harings

Verlag und Druck: tredition GmbH, Hamburg

ISBN
Paperback: 978-3-7469-1484-8
Hardcover: 978-3-7469-1485-5
e-Book: 978-3-7469-1486-2

Prologue

The Second World War is over, the whole of Germany is in ruins and occupied by Allied troops. The general situation in the surrender of the German "Wehrmacht" in May 1945 was so different than at the end of World War I in November 1918. In those days the Reich remained unaffected by enemy troops. Now it was not the case. Tens of millions of German soldiers were also in captivity, the German cities were bombed, tens of millions of refugees from the German eastern territories had to be accommodated. Yet all were glad that the terror came to an end. The hour of refreshing, breathing fetching and hope had begun. The word of the "Zero Hour" could be formulated hardly true in this respect.

With the promulgation of the Basic Law – the new constitution – in 1949 was established the Federal Republic of Germany to the west, while the "German Democratic Republic" was proclaimed in East (in the middle of Germany) With the East is here meant the Soviet occupation zone. The eastern German territories were under Polish administration, which should remain so until 1990. By the Peace Treaty of 1990 these German territories became Polish and Russian territories then. Saarland enjoyed a special status. It became a separate state. Only on 1 January 1957 it became a country of the Federal Republic of Germany.

The first years of the Federal Republic of Germany were called "the years of the Adenauer era". He was the one by whom West Germany was again standing in the world. He was the one who got the last German prisoners of war from the Soviet camps. He was the one who laid the foundation of the German-French friendship, a friendship that in return formed the basis for a European community of values, which subsequently resulted in the establishment of the European Union, of course, after a few precursors. To the European Union, there was still a long way. – Germany was still divided. Two German states claimed the right to represent German interests worldwide.

Then the time has finally come. The reunification. The post-war order that was fixed cemented over 40 years shriveled away within a few months. In Germany, the Berlin Wall fell, the symbol of German division, in Europe raised the "Iron Curtain". People had fought at great sacrifice freedom and democracy. In Germany this happened but without bloodshed.

With the opening of the East German border to the west began for the people in both parts of Germany a new era. Wall and barbed wire they are no longer separated. "We are the people". These words brought down the GDR and led to the reunification in 1990. Father of the reunification was Helmut Kohl.

The implementation of internal unity became after the reunification the most important task of the domestic and economic policy. In East Germany, the reappraisal of the GDR past began. In 1992 right-wing violence against foreigners shocked inter alia in Rostock and Solingen the Federal Republic of Germany. Only one year later changed things in Europe. The map had to be redrawn; Czechoslovakia was divided into two states. In 1996 was then the discussion of the Bonn-saving measures, together with combating unemployment, the second major social and economic policy topic of the year.

In 1997, Germany experienced great floods. The floods on the Odra became a national task. Donations of millions of Euros flowed, 45,000 helpers were on site. Then in 1998 a turning point for Germany represented the deselection of Helmut Kohl, "the Chancellor of German Unity". For the first time, a red-green coalition took power in Bonn. Gerhard Schröder was new Chancellor. He was after Willy Brandt and Helmut Schmidt the third Social Democrat in the Chancellery. With his government takeover ended the era of Helmut Kohl.

1999 confirmed the CDU to have illegally dealt with political donations. Loss of confidence and compensation claims led the party into an existential crisis. – This year Rau became President of Germany. In the second round of voting the delegates of the Federal Assembly elected the former Prime Minister of North Rhine-Westphalia as German President. Then, in 2000, the CDU fell by the donation scandal in a deep crisis. Wolfgang Schäuble and Helmut Kohl resigned from their posts; new leader of the CDU was Angela Merkel.

We write the year 2001. A date shaped the most people like no other. It is September 11. The image of the burning towers of the World Trade Center in New York no one gets this so quickly out of his mind. As a result of the terror it comes to the stock market crash, the US launch attacks on Afghanistan.

In 2002 there is a Flood of the Century in eastern Germany. By this flood 20 people are killed in the cities and towns along the Elbe and its tributaries, whole regions are under water, thousands of homes are destroyed. But despite all the hardship the people in the flooded areas are not alone, because the generosity of the German population is large and with public funds is helped non-bureaucratically. – This year also German soldiers are in Afghanistan. They belong to the "International Security Assistance Force" (ISAF). On 6 March, the first German soldiers are killed in Afghanistan. They die in an accident on an explosive place in Kabul. – On 22 September, the Red-Green government under Gerhard Schröder is confirmed by a narrow margin.

In 2003, a political tragedy happens. Jürgen Möllemann, former political leader of the FDP, dies during a parachute leap. The cause of the death leap has never been solved. Möllemann had come in the weeks before in severe distress. Because of his anti-Israeli statements during the election campaign of 2002, the FDP leadership had separated from him after much hesitation. The Bundestag (German Parliament) had repealed the immunity of the 57-year old and non-attached deputy of parliament only a quarter of an hour before the death leap. Prosecutors of Münster and Düsseldorf let search offices and private rooms on 25 sites in Germany, Spain, Luxembourg and Liechtenstein. Concerning Möllemann was investigated for tax fraud, breach of the Political Parties Act, deception and embezzlement.

In 2004 was the largest EU expansion. 10 states, mainly from Eastern Europe join the EU. – In Germany there was a demonstration against Hartz IV. The Bundestag approved the merger of unemployment benefit and social assistance to unemployment benefit II; thereby was caused a great resentment among the population.

2005 brought many changes. Pope John Paul II dies and a German Cardinal, Joseph Ratzinger, was elected Pope. He takes office as Benedict XVI. – This year there is also a new German Chancellor. Gerhard Schröder missed during the vote on the question of confidence the so-called "Chancellor Majority" of 301 votes of the 601-member parliament. This happened according to his wish! Now CDU/CSU was at the early federal election the strongest force ahead of the SD; but there was only a narrow margin. For CDU/CSU this margin was not enough for the intended coalition with the FDP; but there were also not enough votes for the continuation of the government of Red-Green. Now there was only one possibility, the large coalition of CDU/CSU and SPD. Angela Merkel became chancellor.

In 2006, CDU/CSU and SPD went on developing their plans for a federalism reform and the entry into a health care reform. Both they had previously prevailed in parliament.

With the year 2007 ends this book. It was the year in which Islamist terrorists tried to wreak carnage in Germany and German policemen were killed in Afghanistan. But it was also a great year for Germany, which the G8 summit in Heiligendamm showed.

Germany at the time of the Neanderthals

Buffalo and Original Elephant

The evolution that Darwin described was well known, but no one could foresee that there would be an evolution in German history and politics.

The Germans, a great nation without an own country

We write the year **1946**

The war was over since a few months and the Allies could extract reparations from their occupying zones and that without to fix the level. So there was a dividing line through Germany that was to become a lasting structural border, because the United States and Great Britain put up with the exploitation and plunder of the Soviet zone. The reparations added up, when all was done, to a multiple of that that the west zones had to produce. The west Allies had sacrificed the unity of Germany only to a short moment of the solidary harmony of the victorious powers and they had put up with the sorrow of millions of expellees.

Now the Allies passed over to the daily routine: They settled down in Germany to govern it. Each occupying zone was put in charge of a commander-in-chief, who was only answerable to his government. It was founded the "Control Council" of the Allies to coordinate all matters of the whole of Germany. But this council could pass only unanimous resolutions.

Soon there were differences between the Allies during the foundation of the occupying zones. The French refused to leave the cities Karlsruhe and Stuttgart, which they had taken during their advance in South Germany but which belonged to the U.S.-American zone after the war. Only under massive threat of the Americans they left both cities now. In Thuringia, Saxony and Mecklenburg were American troops, but they left unhesitatingly these countries soon because they belonged to the Soviet zone in the meantime. The Americans also did that, because the Soviets had occupied the whole of Berlin, but Berlin was divided in 4 sectors in the meantime. Now the Americans thought to have the possibility and the right to march into their (own) sector of Berlin, if they would leave Thuringia, Saxony and Mecklenburg.

Berlin should be administrated by the Allies together. But the Soviets had delayed the handing-over of the American, British and French sector. So American and British troops marched into Berlin without Soviet allowance and occupied their sector early in July of the year of 1945. The French followed in August of the same year.

The French had played an odd part within the four-team of the Allies: They were invited neither to the Conference of Yalta nor to the Conference of Potsdam. Charles de Gaulle, the provisional head of the French government, felt treated like a man of secondary importance. Therefore he torpedoed also some decisions of the "Control Council" (only) to prove himself to be an important man there. France held also on to the idea to liquidate Germany for ever and to divide the former German Empire in many little states (so like Saarland!?). France strove also for making the Rhine as German-French frontier, as it was already during the period of the French revolution of the year of 1798. Also the Ruhr (-Pot = the West-German industrial area) should be a French region in future. France had already developed a taste for this region after the "First World War". Now the French government claimed that a final separation of the "Rhine-Westphalian" region together with the "Ruhr (-Pot)" from Germany would be important for the security of France.

The Catholic Church of the Rhineland says: "to pinch coal is allowed." – A coal train from the Ruhr in 1946

The Germans, now a nation without own state, didn't care about the political aims of the victorious powers. They had other problems! The worry of the everyday life weighed too heavily on them. There was a lack of fuel and foodstuffs. Only 60% could the occupied German countries produced themselves. For the difference of the food supply for the inhabitants in the U.S.-American and British zone had every U.S.-American and British taxpayer to pay 600 U.S.-Dollar each year. Another problem was the ruined German currency. The Nazis had financed the war over the money press, now there were 300,000,000,000 RM (Reichsmark) in circulation without equivalent value of merchandise. In Germany circulated additionally to it three currencies: RM (state-salaries were paid out by RM), the currencies of the victorious powers (which the Germans couldn't exchange for RM) and cigarettes, which were the most important currency now, because every German could have all things, which he needed, on the black market, if he paid by cigarettes.

The natural economy was in blossom how in all time of need. Fur coats were exchanged for pots and cans, for a sack of potatoes had the people to pay a piano. The Allies and the German administrative body, which was set up by them, fought in vain with police raids against the black market that was a playground for profiteers and crooks. But the "grey market", which settled the so-called barter transactions, was tolerated. The production didn't function without the exchange of finished products for raw material, but the production had to get going to fulfil the commitment of reparation of the victorious powers.

The Germans pursued with great interest the trial of Nuremberg in spite of considerable every-day cares. The leading élite of the Nazis was accused, as far as the victors could take them into custody. Adolf Hitler, Joseph Goebbels and Heinrich Himmler had evaded the accusation by suicide, as we know.

The Military Court of Justice of Nuremberg

On October 1 of this year the "International Military Court of Justice of Nuremberg" passed sentence on the 24 defendants: 12 of them were sentenced to death by the rope, amongst them was "Reichsmarschall Göring", Foreign Minister Ribbentrop, General Keitel (he was the head of the German armies in the west), the minister of the interior, Frick, the NSDAP-Gau-Leader of Franconia, Julius Streicher, the "Reichskommissar" for the Netherlands, Arthur Seyß-Inquart and "Reichsarbeiterführer" (leader of the worker of the German Empire), Robert Ley. Robert Ley and Hermann Göring escaped their execution by the rope by committing suicide. NSDAP-Reichsleiter (NSDAP-Leader of the Empire) Martin Bormann was sentenced to death "in absence". Hitler's substitute Heß, the minister for economic affairs, Walther Funk, and the commander-in-chief of the German navy, Erich Raeder, were sentenced to life imprisonment; the others, amongst them was the last president of the German Empire, Karl Dönitz, and "Rüstungsminister" (war minister) Albert Speer, got a term of imprisonment of some years. The president of the "German National Bank", Hjalmar Schacht, and the so-called "Hitlers Steigbügelhalter" (Hitler's backer/holder of his stirrup) .Franz von Papen and the head of the "German Broadcasting", Hans Fritsche, were acquitted. After that was the whole of the German nation seized with the denazification and the "re-education" to a "democratic spirit". The Allies tried to filter the minor hanger-on from the principals amongst the Nazis by questionnaires. They wanted to give each hanger-on food for thought for the own investigation of conscience of the joint guilt in the crimes of the National Socialist regime.

The hoarding train of the year 1946

The Soviets made use of the denazification in their zone to carry out the expropriation of the bosses of the German industry and the big landowners. That happened on a large scale in the Russian/Soviet zone of Germany now. By it the Russians/Soviets created the basis for a socialist economy. By the action "Junkerland in Bauernhand" (noble land in farmer's hand) changed 35% of the agriculturally used area of the Soviet occupying zone the hands now. So there were also no obstacles to a nationalization of the economy now. The Soviets had already made provisions and had German communists, who had fled from the Nazis into exile in Moscow, fetched back. On 30 April 1945 landed the "Group Ulbricht" already in Frankfurt on the Odra; the members of this group began immediately with their work after the occupation of Berlin. Walter Ulbricht, the leader of the group, was member of the KPD (Communist Party of Germany) since 1919;

since 1937 he was in Soviet exile. In 1943 he had organized the National Committee "Freies Deutschland" in Moscow that had aimed to bring down Hitler and to finish the war. Also other communists took action now, so in Mecklenburg the "Group Sobottka", in Saxony the "Group Ackermann". "Es muss demokratisch aussehen" (it has to look democratic) said Wolfgang Leonhard, a leading member of the "Group Ulbricht", "aber wir müssen alles in der Hand haben" (but we have to have everything in our hands). But the men around Ulbricht didn't have the intention to carry out democratically all measures; also the representatives of the **"SMAD"** (**S**oviet **M**ilitary **A**dministration of **D**eutschland/Germany) saw to it that it wasn't done. They had advised the German communists in Moscow before and they depended directly on the instructions of the Russian government. The KPD (Communistic Party of Germany) was already admitted as first (new) party in June 1945. On 21 April the KPD under Wilhelm Pieck and the SPD (Social-Democratic Party of Germany) of Middle Germany (Soviet zone) under the leadership of Otto Grotewohl decided the uniting of both parties during a common party conference in (East-) Berlin. The new party bore the name "**S**ozialistische **E**inheitspartei **D**eutschlands" (**SED**/United Socialist Party of Germany) The 800,000 members of the SPD of the Soviet zone and the 600,000 members of the KPD of the Soviet zone were not asked regarding their consent. In West Berlin was only put the uniting of both parties to the vote of the members of the SPD. That happened under the protection of the West Allies. 82% of the members of the SPD of West Berlin voted against a uniting with the communists.

The population of West Germany felt hardly something of the complicated mechanism, by which they were governed. The military government gave the orders as uppermost authority and the Germans had to obey officially these orders. The so-called "official helpers" were chosen; they could also get dismissed on the spot like Konrad Adenauer, the former Mayor of Cologne, who was chased away from his office in the year of 1933. It is true that he became Mayor of Cologne again in May 1945, because his name was in the "white list" of the Allies as adversary of the Nazis, but he was also dismissed again by the British military government in October of the same year. The alleged reason for his dismissal was: incompetence and a lack of performance of his duty.

In January of this year, after the establishment of new parties, were held elections to the municipal councils in Württemberg-Baden that belonged to the U.S.-American zone. Since October were held elections to the parliaments of the countries of the British, French and U.S.-American zone. Now Germany took the administration over more and more in West Germany. Then on December 2 was signed the "Bi-Zone Agreement" by the U.S.-American Secretary of State, James F. Byrnes, and the British Foreign Secretary, Ernest Bevin, in New York (U.S.A.). This agreement came into force on 1 January 1947. The British zone and American zone were economically fused and were to be the core of the new West-German state many months later.

On August 23 founded the British military government in Germany a new country: **North Rhine-Westphalia**; this country was created from the former Prussian province Westphalia and the northern part of the Prussian province Rhineland. On 21 January 1947 was the little country Lippe annexed. The capital of this new country "**NRW**" became Düsseldorf, the seat of the British military government in Germany.

Food Card of the American occupation zone in 1946

On 1 November was founded a new country also in the north of Germany: Lower Saxony. This new country was also created by the British military government. Now the former Prussian province Hannover and the countries Braunschweig (Brunswick), Oldenburg and Schaumburg-Lippe were a part of this new country Lower Saxony. The capital of Lower Saxony became the city Hannover.

On 22 December the German country Saarland was separated from the French-occupied zone and became a separate state within the French economic area. Thus Saarland did also not belong to the new West-German state later and that for many years.

In the end of this year could be also struck the sad balance of the great escape and the expulsion. The matter-of-fact number showed hardly the extent of the horror and the misery. The happenings should be called in closer inspection in spite of that. 220 expellees reached every hour of a day the American-occupied zone in the months January till November of this year. The expellees came from Czechoslovakia (Sudetenland), from there they were "legally expelled", how it was officially called. So 1,500 transports with expellees reach South Germany in these months and that was to be not the end of the expulsion; the last expellees from Czechoslovakia reached Germany in 1952, but now they were called "late re-settlers" (what a scorn!). Also the casualty figure is shocking; during the great escape and the expulsion from East Germany (Silesia, East Prussia and East Pomerania), since 1945, lost more than 2,000,000 German women and children their life, additional to it lost also 1,100,000 German soldiers from East Germany their life during the battles there. In East Germany and Sudetenland were living more than 15,000,000 Germans before the "Second World War" and 3,500,000 of them had lost their lives in the years 1945 and 1946 there, they were killed or died of exhaustion during the run and expulsion. After the first shock by the expulsion the second shock rapidly followed for the expellees by the integration into the new home. Nobody could expect that the inhabitants of West Germany would like to admit the expellees from the east. The people of (West- and Middle) Germany, who were living in ruins, didn't cope with the own problems and now the problems and the misery of the expellees; this was too much for them. The official departments and charitable organizations of West Germany did everything that was possible to make the integration easier. But in spite of that often carelessness and egoism on the one hand and light vulnerability on the other hand led to misunderstanding and hardening in the first time after the war.

For many expellees the odyssey did not yet find an end by assigning of an accommodation. A strong internal migration occurred just in the first years after the war. The separated families had to get brought together again and released prisoners of war were looking for their relatives or women were looking for their released sons, husbands, brothers or fathers. The bringing together of the families was still made difficult by the "Koalitionsverbot" (prohibition of coalitions) of the occupying powers. According to this prohibition it wasn't allowed to form a union of expellees or a self-help organization. Since the most expellees were accommodated in the agricultural regions of the British and American zone, were also missing enough possibilities to work there. The misery was to find no end, because now was still following a hard winter.

Germany and the occupation zones after World War II

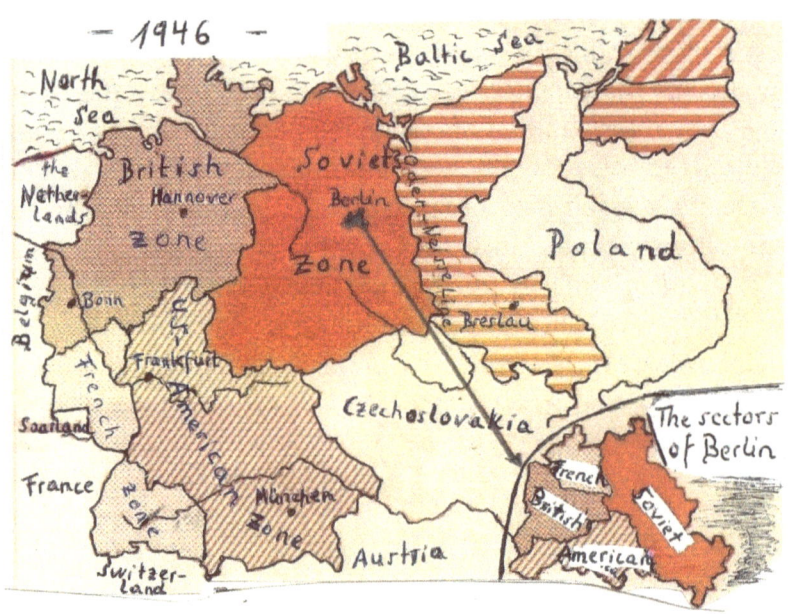

The eastern German territories: East Prussia, East Pomerania, Silesia

 **Under Polish administration**

 **Under Soviet administration**

We write the year **1947**

The winter 1946/47 was terrible for the German population; it was the horrible hunger winter.

The "Trümmerfrauen", a hard work for the recovery of Germany, a hard work for women in the landscape of ruins of Germany; the most men were (still) in captivity.

After the failure of common politics of reparation recouped the Soviet Union its loss from the own zone in Germany and took the goods for the reparation, which the whole of Germany owed Russia, from there. The development of the economic difference between the eastern zone and the western zones went back to this time. Later this difference also contributed to produce a continuous refugee stream from the eastern zone (Soviet/Russian zone) to the western zones.

The Americans knew the ownership of means of production, but the Russians didn't know that because of their communistic system. "Reform of industry" meant to the Americans a decartelization of excessive-concentrated groups of companies and not nationalization, as happened in the Russian occupying zone according to the example of the Soviet Union. Therefore the West-Allies had also cancelled the resolutions of nationalization of the West-German parliaments (Landtage = the parliaments of the German countries). The West-Allies protested against the Soviet taking from the running production of the eastern zone, but that didn't prevent them also from their own taking of coal of the Ruhr (-Pot/region on the Ruhr/river) for the compulsive exports to West Europe.

The lack of coal in the western zones paralyzed the industrial production, which just began to get going. So the German population went hungry and froze as never before in this winter. The "Reichsmark" (RM = the German currency of those days) had lost its value as means of payment and the people could get many vital goods on the black market only.

The division of Germany was a work of the occupying powers; the Germans couldn't prevent them from doing that. But it was a surprise that the Germans willingly cooperated in this work. The Social Democrats (SPD) began with it. During the first conference of all members of the SPD of the whole of Germany, which was already held in September 1945 in Wennigsen close to Hannover, Schumacher, the new leader of the SPD, had not only rejected the claim of leadership of the central committee of Berlin over the whole of Germany, but also each organizational interweaving between the eastern and the western SPD. At the end of this conference Schumacher spoke with Grotewohl about the differences between the SPD-West and the SPD-East and the possible demarcation of both parts of the party.

The Christ-Democrats (CDU/CSU) and the Liberals of West Germany acted similarly. On the first conference of the leading representatives of CDU/CSU from the whole of Germany early in February of this year in Königstein in the Taunus mountains (Hessen) the CDU-chairmen of the eastern zone, Kaiser and Lemmer, tried to get in vain from the party's friends of the western zones that, what the Soviet military governor of the eastern zone, Marshal Sokolovsky, had given them as job on the way: "There is no solution of the German matter without Russia, and there is no breaking asunder of Germany without the Germans". Kaiser and Lemmer had to realize, that they didn't any more have the confidence of their friends of West Germany.

Now the ancient aversion of the West-German province to Berlin and the fear of the Russians grew stronger to the feeling of an indeterminate horror that was what formed the bottom of the attitude of the West-German population towards the Soviet Union in the following decades. The special development of the politics of the east zone and the split of the system of parties was still pressed ahead with the uniting of SPD and KPD into the "Sozialistische Einheitspartei Deutschlands" (**SED**). But also the parties in West Germany were often at variance. So in Bavaria had taken form an independent Christian-democratic party, the **CSU** (**C**hristian-**S**ocial **U**nion), whilst there was the **CDU** (**C**hristian-Democratic Union) in the remainder of Germany. That was to remain till today.

Now in West Germany was existent the bi-zone since some months (France had insisted on an own economic zone in Germany during the first years after the war). The bi-zone got a special weight by its economic success now, especially by the connection with the foreign change of the course of the United States. On January 7 was the American Secretary of State, Byrnes, dismissed and his successor became General Marshall. That was the transition to "containing politics" to the Soviet Union. The head of planning in the (American) State Department, Kennan, had outlined the concept of new politics. Kennan recommended to his government taking steps against a further extension of the Soviet influence by giving financial and economic aid to the free countries for the establishment of settled political conditions and for the securing of the economic stability.

Greece, that was shaken by a civil war, and Turkey, that was hard pressed by the Soviet Union, needed support in this year. On March 12 justified the American president Truman his motion to the Congress for the appropriation of a financial aid for both states. He did it by means of a message, which was designated as "Truman-Doctrine" later: "I believe that the politics of the United States must be to support free nations, which put up resistance to a tried subjection by armed minorities or by hard pressing from outside."

Two days before the promulgation of the "Truman-Doctrine" had started a conference of the foreign ministers of the four victorious powers in Moscow. A compromise in the matter of the forming of a German central administration, the step-by-step appointment of a German government and the basics of a

German constitution seemed to be near at hand now. But then in the matter of reparation it came to a clash of interests. The (American) Secretary of State, George Catlett Marshall, was out to bring about the decision on the German matter any way by the solution of the problem of reparation: Marshall rejected the Soviet claims against Germany to pay a sum of 10,000,000,000 Dollars as reparation. Additional to it the Soviet Union wanted to get materials from the regular (running) production of Germany and to reach a common control of the Ruhr (-region/Ruhr-Pot). But also that was energetically rejected by George Catlett Marshall. Molotov, the Russian Foreign Minister, wanted to measure the West Allies by their faithfulness to treaties and their good will by the fulfilment of the Soviet claims. Now there was reached no agreement. After six weeks the conference adjourned. Marshall announced after the conference, the Americans didn't want to wait to the point of exhaustion for compromises, but they want to start immediately with the stabilization of the European economy.

The international development steered for a confrontation of the super powers and a reorganization of Germany; this meant two (new) German states, a **West-German state** consisting of the British zone with the countries: Schleswig-Holstein, the city state Hamburg and the countries Lower Saxony and North Rhine-Westphalia – the U.S.-American zone with the countries: Württemberg-Baden, Bavaria, Great Hessen and the city state Bremen (with the towns Bremen and Bremerhaven) – the French zone with the countries: Württemberg-Hohenzollern, (South-)Baden and the new country Rhineland-Palatinate (founded by the French occupying power on 30 August 1946, consisting of Rhine-Hessen, the Rhine-Palatinate and the southern part of the former Prussian province "Rhineland", capital is

Mainz), but without Saarland that became an independent state some months later … and an **East German state** consisting of the central German countries Saxony, Mecklenburg and the former Prussian provinces Prussian-Saxony, Anhalt, the western part (and so the larger part) of Brandenburg (the eastern part was administrated by Poland, since 1990 a part of Poland), Thuringia and the western part of Pomerania (the eastern part of Pomerania was also administrated by Poland and is since 1990 a part of Poland). A last attempt to prevent the imminent partition of Germany did the (new) Bavarian Minister President Hans Ehard (CSU). He invited the (new) Minister Presidents of all German countries to a conference in Munich. Ehard was vague about the topic of discussion in his letter of invitation. The Minister Presidents of the east zone demanded during a preliminary discussion on May 5 that the forming of a German central administration by an agreement of the German parties and labour unions had to be as point 1 on the agenda. Ehard wasn't willing to make his colleagues of the east zone, who were under pressure of the SED, concessions. That was the reason now that the Minister Presidents of the east zone already left the conference of Munich before its real starting. The conference was fated from the start no great success, because the Minister Presidents of the French zone had got the instruction by their (French) military government to "don't negotiate about the uniting of all German countries". Also the Minister Presidents of the countries, which were governed by the SPD, had the order of their heads of party to don't negotiate on this subject. So the final statement of the torso-conference didn't have any effect.

The main instrument of the American "containing policy" was the generous credit programme to Europe. The Secretary of State, Marshall, presented his programme for the economic recovery of Europe (Marshall Plan) during a speech in front of students of the university Harvard on June 5· This programme should also be extended to the western zones of Germany. For this it was necessary that the administration of the bi-zone was more effectively shaped. In June were the two-zone-offices, which had worked separately up to now, centralized in Frankfurt/Main. The heads of office were named "directors", to go round to the name "ministers" or "permanent secretary" then. It was allowed the participating governments of the countries of the bi-zone to send one representative each into the executive committee, who had to control the directors. At the head was placed a parliamentary representation, the "Wirtschaftsrat" (economic council with 104 members since February 1948), which was indirectly elected by the parliaments of the countries of the bi-zone and had restricted legislation's competence. In the "economic council" had the middle-class parties a bare majority. They succeeded in placing a CDU-member as director of the "Wirtschaftsrat", who supported the removal of the controlled economy. That happened to the resistance of the SPD. The members of the SPD let consequently the middle-class parties have also the other director's posts now.

The reaction of the Soviet Union to the change in the western zones didn't to be long in coming. The present central administration of the Soviet zone was united into the "Deutsche Wirtschaftskommission" (German economic commission), the preform of the later "DDR-Regierung" (government of the German Democratic Republic/**GDR** = the new East-German state)

The Soviet answer to the "containing policy", which was proclaimed by the U.S.A., was formulated by Zhdanov, a member of the Soviet Politburo, in September. Zhdanov hard attacked the

United States because of their alleged striving for the world domination. He delineated the picture of two camps, which were facing irreconcilably each other. In autumn of this year everybody could feel a fundamental change of the political climate in the eastern zone. The Soviet Union drew the conclusion from the failure of its politics, which was directed to the whole of Germans and prepared the foundation of a "people's-democratic" separate state in the eastern zone. The leading politicians of the middle-class parties were pressed hard to oppose publicly the American politics and to take part in a "Volkskongress für Einheit und gerechten Frieden" (people's congress for unity and just peace). The CDU-chairmen of the Soviet zone, Kaiser and Lemmer, refused to oppose, as a result they were removed from their office by the Soviet military government.

In November the foreign ministers of the four victorious powers had once more a meeting in London (England), at which the American Secretary of State, Marshall, stressed the irreconcilable differences (points of view) between east and west. Then, on December 15, he abruptly broke off the discussions. The only result of this meeting was, France agreed to take part in negotiations about the foundation of a West-German state. Now the foreign ministers of Great Britain and the U.S.A. accepted also the economic union of the Saarland with France, which the French government had already carried out in the meantime, as a token of their good will to France.

1947; SPD, the party for Germans without home!

(Silesians, East Prussians, East Pomeranians and expellees from Sudetenland)

We write the year **1948**

On March 1 was founded the "Bank deutscher Länder" (the new National Bank for West Germany) in Frankfurt. Also on March 1 Professor Ludwig Erhard was elected director of the office for economic of the extended "Wirtschaftsrat" (economic council) of Frankfurt. Erhard was an energetic advocate of the free enterprise, with it he was fully in the line of American politics. On June 18 the three military governors of the western zones directed a currency reform to be done. The new currency should to be valid from 20 June. – The (West-German) currency bore the name "Deutsche Mark" (DM) now. The currency so far, the "Reichsmark" (RM), was devalued in a ration of ten to one; wages, principal and interest were exchanged in a ratio of one to one. Every West-German got 40 DM as "head-rate" on 20 June.

After the currency reform Ludwig Erhard made use of a statutory authority for the change of the price and rationing regulation and abrogated the most provisions concerning this.

The mystery to the success of the currency reform lay in the appeals to an immoral and unlawful behaviour. Factory owners and traders had hoarded large stocks in the last years, which they had withdrawn from the market. Till 20 June no one could also buy most simple things. Now everybody could suddenly buy all things by the new currency and it paid to work hard again. The currency reform, the termination of the rationing and the simultaneously starting "Marshall-Plan-Aid" were going to the initial ignition for the upward trend of the West-German economy.

The currency reform discriminated against the minor people with their savings balances and privileged the owners of objects.

This social injustice was to equalize the "Lastenausgleich" (equalization of burdens) later. But it could really be equalized only a part later then.

The realization of the currency reform gave the Soviet Union cause to the "blockade of West- Berlin"; the Soviets blocked all access roads and waterways from the western zones to West-Berlin and tried by it to starve out the inhabitants of the western part of Berlin. The Soviets spoke of a "technical trouble" only and offered to supply foodstuffs to West-Berlin. On March 20 the Soviet chairman of the "control council", Marshal Vasili Dani-lovich Sokolovsky, had already adjourned the next conference of this council for an indefinite period in protest against the nego-tiations of the west powers about the foundation of a West-German state. During the meeting of March 20 in Berlin he de-manded to be informed about the resolutions of the conference of London, which had been started on February 23 without par-ticipation of the Soviet Union, but the west powers refused to do that. As a result the Soviet delegation left the meeting of the "control council of the Allies". The west Allies were thus not un-prepared taken by the blockade of the roads and waterways to (West-) Berlin. The Americans opened together with the British and French the "airlift" now; that was an aeronautical master-stroke; nobody had seen any possibility to that before. At the height of the crisis landed aeroplanes at regular intervals of some minutes on the airports of West Berlin (seaplanes on the lakes of the western part of Berlin) to provide the inhabitants with foodstuffs, coal and other needed things, also the industry of West Berlin was supplied with replacement parts and all that, which was needed for the production. So it was reached at least that the inhabitants of West Berlin had the most important things for their lives by the airlift. The inhabitants of West Berlin were happy and stood by the West Allies now.

Under the impression of the dramatic situation in Germany, which had come to a head, the Minister Presidents of the western zones had a meeting on 1 July in Frankfurt. Now in Frankfurt they were to get the order by the three military governors to found a (new West-) German state and to accept the guidelines to a bill of a (new) German constitution (Frankfurter Dokumente/Documents of Frankfurt). The Minister Presidents discussed their further line of action at a conference close to Koblenz (town on Rhine/French zone) now. There they had objections to a cooperation regarding a partition of Germany. Now the vote of the elected Mayor of West Berlin, Ernst Reuter (SPD), was decisive. Reuter, the elected but not certified Mayor of West Berlin, implored his colleagues, the Minister Presidents of the West German countries, to venture on a new state beginning in the western part of Germany, because then there would be only a chance to join again with the countries of the eastern zone (in the middle of Germany) and perhaps also with the eastern part of Germany, the countries Silesia, East Pomerania and East Prussia, which were under the administration of Poland and Russia in those days. The Minister Presidents reached an agreement about the convocation of a "Parlamentarischer Rat" (parliamentary council), which should be elected by the "Landtage" (parliaments of the countries) and should draw up the text of a "Grundgesetz" (basic constitutional law); the majority of the parliaments should decide on the passing then.

On the 1st of July the Soviets discontinued their cooperation in the four-power headquarters of Berlin. That was the end of a common administration for Berlin. East Berlin was administrated separately by the Soviets now.

On the 12th of July the last German prisoners-of-war were released by Great Britain. – On July 15 introduced Saarland an own nationality. The inhabitants of Saarland were no longer Germans by it. Saarland was a sovereign state now and also didn't any more belong to the French (occupied) zone.

On the 2nd of August U.S.-American, British and French government representatives had a talk with the Soviet dictator Stalin and Foreign Minister Molotov. The Soviet Union agreed to bring the blockade of West Berlin to an end, but that only if a common currency reform in all zones of the four occupying powers would be realized. But it was reached no agreement on this matter. On August 10 began the committee of the West-German countries with the preparatory discussions of a German basic constitutional law (Grundgesetz) on the island Herrenchiemsee in Lake Chiem/see in Bavaria. On August 12 was West Berlin still blockaded and the aeroplanes of the West Allies took each day 4,500 tons of goods to the blockaded city.

On the 13th of August Gebhard Müller, a member of the party CDU, became new president of the country Württemberg-Hohenzollern. This country belonged to the French zone. The first president of this new country was Lorenz Bock (CDU); he died some days ago. On August 15 were started the elections in the "Landtagen" (parliaments of the countries) of the bi-zone (American and British zone) for the members of the "Parlamentarischer Rat" (parliamentary council). The polling for this council was to come to an end on August 30. Only some days later the Soviet military police had carried out an illegal police raid in the U.S.-American sector of Berlin. The cause for this raid was, to redress the black market in the whole city. 2,500 persons were arrested by the Soviets during this action. – On August 20 was abrogated the compulsory passport between the French zone and the bi-zone. By it was abolished the controls on the border between both zones. Up to now were the (German) inhabitants of the French zone holders of a passport in French/German language and the inhabitants of the bi-zone holders of a passport in English/German language. At the crossing point between both zones the Germans had to present always this passport if they crossed the border. Now the inhabitants of West Germany were happy because they were inhabitants of the united "three zones" without controls on the borders between the western zones and in Rhineland the people were singing: "Wir sind die Eingeborenen von Trizonesien …" (We are the aborigines of Trizonesia … / = tri/three zones)

On the 30th of August representatives of the west powers had (again) a meeting with the Soviet Foreign Minister Molotov in Moscow. Now they agreed to continue the administrative consultations about Berlin by the military commanders of this city. After that the military commanders of Berlin started their negotiations one day later.

On the 1st of September the parliamentary council constituted itself in Bonn. There were 65 delegates from 11 "Landtagen" of West Germany; additionally 5 delegates from (West-) Berlin came to Bonn, but they had only an advisory function. This constituent assembly should draw up the constitution for (the new state) West Germany. Konrad Adenauer (CDU) was elected chairman of this constituent assembly on September 15.

There was a tragic incident quite near the "Reichstagsgebäude" (building of the former German parliament) on the 9th of September in Berlin. In the British sector Soviet sentries fired at 250,000 demonstrators, who protested against the Soviet measures in East Berlin. One person was killed and 22 were injured during this action. That was the first demonstration against the Soviet Union on German ground. Five days later went representatives of the West Allies to Moscow again to continue the talk about Berlin with the Soviet Foreign Minister Molotov. But on September 26 this talk was broken off again, because the Soviet Union didn't want to end the blockade against West Berlin. Now the western Allies announced that they will take the affair "Berlin" to the UNO.

On the 14th of October the parliamentary council (Parlamentarischer Rat) announced the new name for the future West-German state; the name should be "Bundesrepublik Deutschland" (Federal Republic of Germany).

On the 5th of November the third airbase for the airlift in West-Berlin, it was the airport Tegel, was opened. The Soviet Union threatened some days later the West Allies with the shooting down of their aeroplanes, if they would fly outside the air corridor to West-Berlin.

On the 30th of November the first Mayor of East-Berlin, the Soviet sector of Berlin, was elected. It was Friedrich Ebert, a member of the (new) party **SED** (**S**ozialistische **E**inheitspartei **D**eutschlands). The Soviet considered with it East-Berlin to be an independent city. Friedrich Ebert immediately formed after his election a "Magistrat" (= administration/government of the city) On December 7 followed West-Berlin with the re-election of Ernst Reuter as Mayor of West-Berlin.

On the 11th of December a new liberal party was founded in Heppenheim/Hessen. This new party named itself "Freie **Deutsche Partei**" (**FDP**), the president became Prof. Theodor Heuss.

On the 28th of December the United States, Great Britain, France, the Netherlands, Belgium and Luxembourg signed an agreement about the common control over the German heavy industry of the region Ruhr(-Pot). The Germans had not yet rights to rule over their country, also they were still waiting for an own sovereign state.

Hunger and no housing

Ground zero in Germany, "Improvisation" was the keyword after the war. It was important for everyone to get a "Dach über dem Kopf" (roof over the head) again, because the most Germans didn't have a housing. The Germans were living in ruins, in cellars or in rusting sheet metal cabins. Now they start to build provisional accommodations. Building material they found in the ruins. In October 1945 the Allies gave the order to clear the rubble mass away. Because the most German men were in captivity, the women had to do this work. The so-called "Trümmerfrau" (rubble woman) was born. They knocked off the mortar from the bricks by simple trowels or other tools. They became by it the symbol of the German recovery. But the new built rooms weren't enough, millions of fugitives flocked to West Germany; they had to leave their homes in the east of Germany or were coming from Bohemia and Moravia (Sudetenland/the former German part of the Czech. Rep.) Therefore the Allies of the western zones settled this problem by a law, "one room for one family" (= 4 persons). That caused resentments against the fugitives. But worst of all was the hunger. Germany had lost its granary in the east. More people in the west had to be supported from a smaller agricultural area. In 1945 began already the catastrophe. The British commander-in-chief in Germany, General Montgomery, announced that a German had to get 1,500 calories each day. In April 1946 was found that every inhabitant of the U.S.-American zone get 1,275 calories each day, every inhabitant of the British zone 1,040 calories and every inhabitant of the French zone 927 calories each day (in the Soviet zone least of all, but there was also missing a number) The UNO had quoted 2,550 calories as subsistence level. – In the British zone were more than 70% of the pupils underfed; many deficiency symptoms spread epidemically out, as tuberculosis. Every day died 200 persons of starvation in Germany, but without the support from the United States and Great Britain would be died more persons. Then, 1946/47, the "cold winter" came. Now many people were killed by the "white death" (= snow and frost). In many cities and towns the people could warm themselves in halls or public cabins, but there wasn't enough for all the persons. So they died in the streets. Also the quota of calories was reduced now, so in Hamburg for every inhabitant only 800 calories each day, in Essen (Ruhr-Pot) 740 calories each day. Now every inhabitant of West Germany had also claim to a shirt every ten years, a suit every forty years and only every third dead person had claim to a coffin.

Now began the time of "Care-Packages" from the United States. The inhabitants of West Germany got more than one million packages from the Americans every month. They could find in them all that what they needed, food, chocolate, cigarettes and so on. The head of the U.S.-American military government of

Great Hessen had an originally idea as thanks for the American support: he served his guests from the United States a **"big dinner in German style"**: spare coffee (the so-called **"Muckefuck"** = coffee made from barley), water soup, 2 potatoes boiled in their jackets and 5 grams of margarine; that **was the typical dinner of the Germans in those days**. But many Germans were also happy; they had a little garden in the ruins, on their balconies, in their cellars or also in the fields near the towns. There they had chickens and could plant vegetable and fruits.

During the coldness of the winter 1946/47 the Germans were also missing coals, they had to produce only for the victorious powers. Therefore they pinched the (own) coal from the railway carriages. The bishop of Cologne, Cardinal Frings, gave even his absolution for coal robbery: "Wir leben in Zeiten, da in der Not auch der einzelne das wird nehmen dürfen, was er zur Erhaltung seines Lebens und seiner Gesundheit notwendig hat" (We are living in a time, in which everyone can take that, what he needs for the preservation of his life and health) … In Rhineland this coal robbery was called "fringsen", which was a "good" verb, derived from the word Frings.

Two German states

We write the year **1949**

On 24 January the representatives of the parliamentary council and the heads of the government of the West-German countries created a preparation's committee for the coordination of the political administration of the western zones. Only one day later confirmed the **SED** (**S**ozialistische **E**inheitspartei **D**eutschlands/Socialist United Party of Germany) the adaptation of its politics to the politics of the Communistic Party of the Soviet Union. That happened at the first party conference of the SED in the Soviet zone.

On 3 February the members of the Parliamentary Council of West Germany agreed to enter, apart from the eleven countries of the western zones, also West Berlin into the preamble to the constitution (basic law) Then on 11 February, the bill of the basic law to West Germany was passed by the Parliamentary Council.

On 19 March the "Volksrat" (people's council) of the countries of the Soviet zone passed an own basic law. By it Germany was finally divided. – The western Allies declared the (new) currency of the Soviet zone null and void in West Berlin one day later, whilst the (new) currency of West Germany (DM) was also adopted in West Berlin. The currency reform was done by it in West Germany and West Berlin.

On 8 April the West Allies agreed on an occupying statute to the three western zones in Washington (U.S.A.) By it the occupying regime got a contractual basis. A few days later were also the last criminals of the Nazi-regime sentenced by the U.S.-American Military Court of Justice in Nuremberg/Nürnberg. 19 criminals got long imprisonments between 4 and 25 years.

On 15 April the military governors of the western zones authorized the "Parlamentarische Rat" (Parliamentary Council) to enact
a "Bundeswahlgesetz" (election law to a federal republic). The
administrative body of the Soviet zone cut off the same day the
telephone connection between the U.S.-American zone and the
east zone (Soviet zone).

On 23 April was corrected the German-Belgian frontier line in
the south of Aachen (the town of Charles the Great). Belgium
got by it 20 km² (square kilometres) of the former German Empire. Also the frontier line between the Netherlands and West
Germany was corrected. The Netherlands got 90 km² of the former German Empire.

On 4 May representatives of the three West Allies had a meeting
with representatives of the Soviet Union in New York (U.S.A.).
There they agreed about the close of the blockade against West
Berlin now. On May 12 came the blockade of West Berlin finally
to an end then.

On 12 May the "Parlamentarische Rat" (Parliamentary Council)
passed the (new) basic law of West Germany (the constitution of
the future state) with 53 to 12 votes. Two days later voted the
most delegates of the "Parlamentarische Rat" for Bonn as capital
of the "Federal Republic of Germany". 33 delegates voted for
Bonn, 29 for Frankfurt on Main (river). Especially the SPD wished
Frankfurt as (new) capital.

On 21 May all West German countries, with the exception of
Bavaria, ratified the (new) basic law. But the Bavarian "Landtag"
(parliament) accepted the legal binding of this law, because also
the most of the other ten countries of West Germany (Schleswig-Holstein, Bremen, Hamburg, Lower Saxony, North Rhine-

Westphalia, Great Hessen, Rhineland-Palatinate, Württemberg-Hohenzollern, Württemberg-Baden, South-Baden) had accepted this basic law. Then on 23 May was signed the basic law by the Minister Presidents, the presidents of the eleven "Landtage" and the delegates of the "Parlamentarische Rat" (with the exception of two delegates of the Communistic Party of West Germany). The (new) state "Bundesrepublik Deutschland" (Federal Republic of Germany/West Germany) was born. On 30 May the Soviet zone followed with an own (East-) German state. There was the constitution of the "Volksrat" of the countries of the Soviet zone announced as national constitution of the (new) state "**D**eutsch-le **D**emokratische **R**epublik" (**DDR**/German Democratic Republic). By it were existent two German states now (with Saarland and Austria even 4 German states), in the west and in the middle of Germany, whilst Poland and Russia administrated the east (territories) of Germany. Now the most people of the world designated more and more the middle of Germany for "East Germany".

The close of the work of the "Parlamentarische Rat" in May was also the starting shot to the beginning of the electoral battle for the first "Bundestag" (Lower House of the West German parliament). Also the inhabitants of West Berlin wanted to take part in the election, but the three west Allies rejected that because West Berlin was no part of the "Federal Republic of Germany" (West Germany), it belonged to the United States, Great Britain and France as separate German city. So the electoral battle was started without participation of the inhabitants of West Berlin. Main subject of the electoral battle was of course the arguments for the economic policy. The Social-Democrats castigated the market economy of Prof. Erhard as class struggle from above and demanded planned economy and nationalization of the basic industry. Erhard was apart from Adenauer, the leading candidate of the CDU, star speaker of the party during the electoral battle. The CDU had made Erhard's theses for the "social market economy" its own. At the central electoral meeting of the CDU in Heidelberg Adenauer proclaimed: "The point of this battle is, whether (West-) Germany is governed like a Christian or is governed socialistically. The socialism cannot form a bank against the communism". At the same time annoyed the chairman of the SPD the Catholic workers of North Rhine-Westphalia, whose votes had to be decisive for the result of the election.

The result of the "Bundestagswahl" (election to the Lower House of the West German parliament) of August 14 was a bitter disappointment for the SPD and its chairman Schumacher. The CDU/CSU became the strongest political power of West Germany by a lead of 500,000 votes. During the polling were cast 24,500,000 votes, the CDU/CSU got 7,400,000 votes (31%), the SPD 6,900,000 votes (29.2%), the FDP 2,800,000 votes (11.1%), the KPD 1,400,000 votes (5.9%), the DP 900,000 votes (4.0%) and all the other parties together 4,000,000 votes (18.2%). Short time after the polling succeeded Konrad Adenauer in swearing the leading politicians of CDU/CSU by a forming of a small coalition with the FDP and DP under his leadership as chancellor.

Konrad Adenauer, the first chancellor of the Federal Republic of Germany (West Germany)

The main argument of Adenauer against a great coalition with the SPD was: the voters had decided in favour of the "Social Market Economy" by a large majority and the future policy of the government had to comply with the decision of the majority.

On 7 September "Bundestag" (parliament of West Germany/Lower House) and "Bundesrat" (Upper House/parliament of the representatives of the countries of West Germany) constituted themselves. Now the "Bundesversammlung" (Assembly of the deputies of the West German parliament/Lower House and representatives from the countries of West Germany) elected also Prof. Theodor Heuss, who was chairman of the FDP (Liberal Party), President of the Federal Republic of Germany by the majority of the middle-class parties. Then the "Bundestag" elected Konrad Adenauer, who was chairman of the **CDU** (**C**hristian-**D**emocratic **U**nion/the Christian Party of West Germany), chancellor. Five days later could the first chancellor of West Germany present his cabinet of the "small coalition". By it was coming the time to the three west powers to transfer the government power to the new state, to liquidate their military governments in West Germany and to put into force the "occupying statute", which was agreed in the spring time. This "occupying statute" reserved the right of the three victorious west powers to keep the office of foreign politics, the office of foreign economy, the office of demilitarization, the office of security, the "Office for the Protection of the Constitution", the office for the abolition of cartels, the office for the handling of the reparations and the right to intervene any time in the (West-) German legislation. The west powers had also withdrawn the control of the important industrial zone "Ruhr-Pot" from West Germany by the "Ruhrstatut" (Statute of Ruhr). That happened in favour of France, Belgium, the Netherlands and Luxembourg. So the communists were right with their assertion that they branded the regime of the west powers as colonial statute.

Theodor Heuss, the first President of the Federal Republic of Germany (West Germany)

On 7 October was also officially proclaimed the "**Deutsche Dem**okratische **R**epublik" (**DDR**/the constitution was already announced in May, as we know) as sovereign state in the middle of Germany. The first Minister President (Prime Minister) of the DDR became Otto Grotewohl, who emphasized immediately his friendship with the Soviet Union and admitted the Oder-Neisse line as frontier between (East) Germany and Poland.

It was the same question that arose for the (new) West German government in this year, which also arose for the government of the former German Empire in the year of 1919: Should the new (West) German government pursue a policy of fulfilment or call a national resistance? Adenauer didn't have forgotten the lesson of the "Ruhrkampf" (struggle of Ruhr) of the year of 1923, resistance was useless, didn't have a sense. He supported the demands of the occupying powers to cooperate closely with them and to come to a fundamental change of the relationship with France.

This policy was no tactic of Adenauer. The West German Republic should be firmly bound to the side of the west powers by a European integration, which narrowed more and more. Adenauer, the first chancellor of the West German Republic, declared in his first policy statement that the Germans belonged by birth and convictions to the western world. The way to the freedom would be, to extend piece by piece the liberties and competence in agreement with the "High Commission of the Allies" (The new West German Republic wasn't yet a sovereign state in all spheres). Adenauer confessed also to the reunification of Germany, protested against the Oder-Neisse line as German east frontier and laid claim to the West German government to speak alone for the whole of Germany as a democratic legitimate government. By means of the domestic programme of the government of Adenauer was planned the continuation of the social market economy, tax relief for boosting the production and measures for getting over the worst social plight.

The violent social-democratic opposition to the programme of the government was a foregone conclusion. It is true that Schumacher was for the West German state and the western orientation from the beginning, but he wanted only to start the cooperation with the west powers and the European integration on the basis of equal rights, also he wanted to defy concessions from the west powers if necessary. His big worry was that by the unreasonableness of the victorious powers could be again provoked a national opposition in Germany. But then this opposition was to find itself again in the SPD in contrast to the time after 1919.

The most urgent problem to the new government of West Germany was the discontinuance of the dismantling, of which continuance obstructed the recovery and made the cooperation with the west powers more difficult. Therefore Adenauer wrote to the conference of the three foreign ministers of the west Allies in Paris that the (West-) German government would agree to cooperate in the "Ruhrbehörde" (Administrative Body of Ruhr/the official office of the West Allies for business of the region on the Ruhr) and would also support the job of the military office of security of the three powers. After the conference of Paris, Adenauer was invited by the "High Commissioners" of the West Allies to come to Mount Peters/berg close to Bonn. There was to take place three rounds of negotiations now. The result of these meetings was the "Petersberger Abkommen" (Agreement of Petersberg) of November 22, 1949. It was the first treaty of the new West German state: the "Federal Republic of Germany" bound itself for the cooperation in the "Ruhrbehörde" and for the support of the "Sicherheitsamt" (office of security). The West Allies agreed in return to it to cancel 18 factories of the petro-chemistry and steel industry from the list of dismantling and to stop completely the dismantling in (West-) Berlin. Now the participation of the "Federal Republic of Germany" in all organizations of the European cooperation was determined as common goal according to this agreement.

The SPD-opposition heavily attacked Adenauer, because he had agreed to the start of the European integration on the basis of the inequality of the Germans and had also passed the "Bundestag" (West German parliament) over at this decision. Adenauer drove grossly the Social-Democrats during the night-session of the "Bundestag" between 24 and 25 November, when he read out a consenting announcement of the "German Federation of Labour Unions" and put the question to the SPD, whether the members of the SPD would prefer to continue the dismantling to the bitter end. After shouts from the left side: "Das ist nicht wahr! Sprechen Sie als deutscher Kanzler? (That's not true! Do you speak as German chancellor?), called Schumacher, the chairman of the SPD, behind the following comment: "Bundeskanzler der Alliierten!" (Chancellor of the Allies!)

We write the year **1950**

The SPD's criticism of the government of West Germany was provoked again in the spring time of this year by the form, in which the integration of West Germany happened within the "Council of Europe". The government of West Germany had to apply for a less entitled member of the "Council of Europe" and had also to accept that also Saarland became member of this council. France wanted to demonstrate by it that Saarland wasn't a part of Germany, that Saarland was a sovereign state (but under French control).

The French-German relationship had reached its low, but a French initiative campaigned for a new European start now: The "Schuman-Plan" for the fusion of the French and German coal and steel industry, the foundation of the "Montan Union". Robert Schuman (French Prime Minister 1947/48 and minister many times over) belonged to the convinced supporters of a European Union. His great fear was that the Germans could obtain one day again the predominance over the French. The fear was still kindled by the English and Americans in this spring time, who urged more and more the French government to consent to a new increase of the German steel production, whilst there was a trend towards overproduction in France. Schuman let himself work out a model for surmount of the steel crisis by the French industrial planner Jean Monnet. Monnet proposed to put the coal and steel industry of West Germany and other European states in charge of the administration of a super-national high authority with regard to the price development, the investments and the foreign trade. Schuman stated unchanged this model with the policy statement of May 9. He gave reasons for this proposal with it that by the fusion of the industries of Montan (= coal mining and steel industry) the contrast between Germany and France, which was some hundred years old, will get over, that a war between both states will be impossible in future and that this project means the first step on the way to an "European Federation".

The German chancellor, Konrad Adenauer, welcomed the proposal of Schuman the same day, but only Italy, Belgium, the Netherlands and Luxembourg were willing to cooperate with France and West Germany in the "Montan Union", the first European federation.

No event had so lasting effect on the political development of the Federal Republic of Germany as the outbreak of the war in Korea. The invasion of South Korea by troops of North Korea seemed to signal that the "international communism" was prepared to pass over from the cold war to the hot war. The American atomic bomb seemed to have lost its deterrent effect. Now the Americans spoke freely, what their General Staff had given to understand only on the quiet since 1948: West Europe couldn't be defended without a new West German army. Everybody knew the importance of (West-) Germany, therefore meant also an invasion of communist troops from the east to West Germany a direct military conflict with the U.S.A.

Chancellor Adenauer had already striven for rearmament since 1948. He thought: West Germany must rearm to avert the Soviet threat and to become a sovereign state. A state without army would be at best a protectorate of foreign powers and if the worst would come to the worst their battlefield. Adenauer offered of his own accord the rearmament without to wait for an official inquiry of the west powers, without consent of the West German government and without discussion in the "Bundestag" (Lower House of the West German parliament). On 29 August he addressed two memoranda to the American High Commissioner McCloy. In the first document he demanded of the west powers a security guarantee and offered at the same time the activating of German troops. In the second document he demanded in return for new German Armed Forces the abolition of the "occupying statute" by a settlement by treaty and the abolition of the state of war with Germany.

The foreign ministers of the three west powers negotiated intensively on the rearmament of West Germany at their conference in New York. The foreign ministers confirmed once more the security guarantee of the west powers for the Federal Republic of Germany and West Berlin and conceded to the West German Republic and West Berlin to activate a "Bundesgrenzschutz" (Federal Border Police), also they promised to put in view a revision of the "occupying statute". But the French foreign minister said clearly "no" to rearmament of West Germany. The occupation of France by the German army had the

French in their fresh mind, the threat from the east had against that only a theoretical effect on them.

The first German resistance to the intended rearmament came from the own government. The ministers of the Federal Republic got to know about the sending of the security memorandum before their cabinet meeting of August 31. Gustav Heinemann, who had jurisdiction over security affairs and became president of West Germany some years later (1969 – 1974), entered a protest against this memorandum. He was for the repulse of communistic encroachments by means of the police and against a rearmament, which could make impossible a reunification. Now Heinemann announced his resignation. But the other members of the cabinet accepted the arbitrary act of Adenauer. In the public the "einsame Entschlüsse" (lonely decisions) of the chancellor turned to a stereotype of the criticism of Adenauer.

A new army was the last the Germans wanted to have in this year. They strove for better eating, better residing and buying of new household effects. The first reaction was a general "Ohnemich Stimmung" (without myself mood). For the young generation, which had just received a re-education, could have the call to the barracks no attraction. The war generation was still looking for the connection with the civilian life and couldn't understand why representatives of the past time were put in so many important positions.

The Federal Republic of Germany had been founded as economic state. The internal success of West Germany and its success in the contest of the both world systems on German ground had to depend on the success, whether West Germany succeeded in offering economically attractive living conditions for its inhabitants. The economic conception of the (West-) German minister for economic affairs, Prof. Ludwig Erhard, aimed at the restoration of a productive export industry. Public funds weren't available for the expansion of the production plants, there were only available the credits of the "Marshall-Plan". But the West German government granted lowering of the income tax and possibilities of write-down to the companies. The self-financing of the companies was realized over prices. The production had an upward tendency. An odd fanaticism seemed to be in its initial stages to unite labourers and companies. The other side of this unplanned economic growth met above all with the criticism of the labour unions: the rising number of unemployment and the structural unemployment in the regions, which were far-off from industries and occupied on above-average with fugitives. In this year the labour unions kept also back the demand for salary increase because there were already more than 2,000,000 unemployed persons in West Germany; therefore the labour unions didn't want that the number of unemployment was also rising more. Erhard's experiment had perhaps failed, if there wouldn't have been the development of the world economy for the benefit of the West Germans. The war of Korea produced an effect on the economic growth, which seized the whole of the world economy (Korea boom). The West German production was on the increase of 20% and the increase of export reached also a two-digit number in the following years.

The situation in the middle of Germany (in the German Democratic Republic/DDR) was far worse than in West Germany. In the DDR (GDR) was the production running in the sense of the communistic planned economy, that was, the Germans in the **German Democratic Republic** (**GDR**/DDR) had also to produce (exclusively) for the Soviet Union.-- On 19 July became the Federal Republic of Germany (West Germany) and Saarland members of the Council of Europe officially.

On 6 June the DDR had recognized the Oder-Neisse-line as final west frontier of Poland, whilst the people of West Germany were still hoping that the east of Germany (Silesia, East Pomerania and East Prussia) could be a part of Germany again one day. The DDR (GDR) gave also up the claims to the "Sudetenland" and approved the expulsion of more than 3,000,000 Germans of Bohemia and Moravia (today Czech. Rep.) – On 24 July, Walter Ulbricht was elected secretary-general of the DDR; that happened at the conference of the new founded central committee of the German Democratic Republic. On 29 September became the DDR member of the council of the communistic countries for mutual economic aid (Comecon)

Europarat (Council of Europe)

On 5 May 1949 was the Council of Europe founded by 10 European states. The first members of this organization were: Belgium, the Netherlands, Luxembourg, Denmark, France, Great Britain, Ireland, Italy, Norway and Sweden. Later joined the following states: Greece, Turkey, Iceland, Austria, Cyprus, Switzerland, Malta, Portugal, Spain, Liechtenstein, Saarland and the Federal Republic of Germany.

The Council of Europe is a forum for discussions of European problems and for the promotion of common interests and has its seat in Strasbourg (Alsace). The organs of the Council of Europe (not European Council that is another organization and was founded 1974) are: Committee of Minister, Parliamentary Assembly, secretary-general office, orderly committees. The Parliamentary Assembly, of which members were elected by the national parliaments but forms political and not national groups (Christian-democratic, socialist, liberal), has three times a meeting each year and can give only recommendations. The Committee of Minister, the foreign ministers were members of it, decides on passing the recommendations of the participants of these meetings on the member states then. The members of the Council can make important decisions only unanimously and little important decisions with two third majority. The focal points of the Council of Europe are: protection of the human rights, humanizing of the working conditions, adaptation of the rights, common protection and utilization of the natural riches, adaptation of the educational policy, of contacts in the interest of education, labour and holiday.

We write the year **1951**

The unemployment was falling off in this year in West Germany, the economic upswing began. Prof. Erhard could let celebrate himself as "father of the West German economic miracle". The economic success legitimized the restoration of the free enterprise.

The first restoration was beyond the economic order a characteristic feature of the early era of Adenauer. This feature showed itself in a special clearness in the sectors of reparation and restoration of the sphere of the (professional) officials. The first claim to aid and reparation had the victims of NS-crimes, especially Jews, who had survived the terrible NS-regime.

Adenauer professed ceremoniously himself to be for the restoration: that happened in front of the "Bundestag" on 27 September.

This year began the disputes between the United States and France because of the French refusal of a (new) German army. The American government didn't want to accept the French veto and strengthened its pressure on France. René Pleven, the French Prime Minister (1950-1952), had already proposed the forming participation in October of the year of 1950. The proposal seemed to designate a continuation of the European integration, which was started by the "Treaty of Montan Union" on 18 April of this year (this Treaty of Montan Union, a treaty for coal and steel, was signed by France, West Germany, Italy, Belgium, the Netherlands and Luxembourg) After many previous exploratory meetings on the talks were started the negotiations about a forming of an "European Defensive Community" of six states of the "Montan Union" in this year in Paris. In the autumn of this year began parallel to it the negotiations of the "High Commissioners" of the three west powers with the government of West Germany about the cancellation of the "occupying statute". That happened on Mount Peters/berg close to Bonn, the capital of West Germany. The west powers had revised the "occupying statute" as previous action during the spring time of this year and permitted the Federal Republic of Germany to set up a Foreign Ministry and a Diplomatic Service. The west powers had also cancelled the industrial restrictions and the control over the foreign trade and had declared the end of the state of war with Germany. Signs of the good will of the west powers were also the return of the town Kehl on Rhine and the island Heligoland to West Germany.

In the autumn of this year was the focus of the political discussion the subject "reunification". All parties of the "Bundestag", with the exception of the communists, had already demanded free elections in the whole of Germany in the year of 1950. The call for freedom of the "Paulskirche" (Paul's Church) of Frankfurt of the year of 1848 sounded still in it. In 1950 nobody could expect that the Soviet Union would agree to an election. But on 15 September of this year contacted surprisingly the Prime Minister of the GDR, Otto Grotewohl (1949 – 1964), the government of West Germany and suggested an all-German discussion of holding free all-German elections. The government of West Germany rejected this suggestion for the reason that the government of the DDR (GDR) wouldn't be democratically legitimized. But the Social Democrats put the (West German) government under pressure to realize the project of an "all-German election". Also this subject suited the SPD (Social Democratic Party of Germany) fine, because this party saw its hope dashed in the economic policy and was split on the issue of rearmament. Schumacher had rejected the German contribution to a "European Defensive Community", because this community would be too weak and the members of this community would also discriminate against the Germans. But the SPD was successful with the slogan "Nie wieder Krieg" (never again war) during the elections to the parliaments of the West German countries. In the matter of reunification by free elections the SPD could take a solid action against the hesitating government of West Germany.

In November petitioned the West German government for a ban on the KPD (Communistic Party of Germany) by the "Bundesverfassungsgericht" (Federal Constitutional Court) in Karlsruhe; that was a spectacular occurrence especially in this phase, because nobody could introduce oneself an all-German election without the participation of the KPD.

On 9 December was held a plebiscite in the south German countries Württemberg-Baden, Württemberg-Hohenzollern and (South-) Baden; the reason was: foundation of a new (united) country in the south. 69.7% voted for the uniting of these three countries; thus was now founded a new country in the south of Germany, Baden-Württemberg with the capital Stuttgart (the so-called "Daimler City", or the city with "Mercedes star")

We write the year **1952**

During the spring time were made two international treaties by the West German government, in Paris the treaty about the "European Defensive Community" and in Bonn the "Deutschlandvertrag" (Treaty of Germany). By the "Deutschlandvertrag" was regularized the relationship between the three west powers and West Germany and the return of the sovereignty to West Germany, but that only with reservations. The three powers had reserved all rights relating to Germany as a whole, relating to Berlin and to the deployment of troops. Common goal of the parties to this agreement was according to the treaty: reunification of Germany, the integration of West Germany into the "European Community", the conclusion of a peace treaty (here was Germany free to do it) and the postponement of the issue of the German east frontier. As known, Silesia, East Pomerania and East Prussia were occupied and administrated by Poland and Russia, but these territories were still parts of Germany.

Adenauer, the West German chancellor, had only informed his cabinet and the coalition partners in broad outline of the progress of the negotiations and the contents of the agreements of Paris and Bonn to prevent the government from saying something against these agreements before the treaties were really made. The members of the government also didn't have time to look into the treaties. On 26 May was the "Deutschlandvertrag" already singed in Bonn and on 27 May in Paris the treaty about the "European Defensive Community".

On 10 March the Soviet government had reported to the west powers by means of a note. By this note proposed the Soviet Union immediate negotiations about the reunification of Germany and the conclusion of a peace treaty. The principles of a peace treaty should be: freedom of alliance for the whole of Germany, the right to an own national army, the recognition of the Oder-Neisse-line as German east frontier (= renunciation of Silesia, East Pomerania and East Prussia for ever) and the withdrawal of all occupying troops within of one year. That was an offer of the Soviet Union with the greatest content. The only reaction of the government of West Germany sounded optimistically. One minister of the Federal Republic of Germany demanded a careful examination, but Adenauer reacted against the note in the way of flat refusal. On 14 March he announced during a speech in the town Siegen (North Rhine-Westphalia) that the note of the Soviet Union would be only a manoeuvre to put West Germany to trouble, the offer of an own national army only a "Fetzen Papier" (scrap of paper), only a policy of strength would produce the conditions for real talks with Moscow. The Soviet note didn't suit the west powers at all, because West Germany should be the "last stone of a European defensive building". Immediate negotiations of the four powers had showed that the west powers wouldn't have been willing to extend the independence and equality, which they had planned for their new ally, also to a non-aligned all-German state.

Adenauer outlined the picture of a policy of alliance in front of the parliamentary party CDU/CSU; this policy should connect the issue of reunification with the freeing of the east European states from the Soviet supremacy. But soon the resistance within the ruling parliamentary party concentrated on a clause in the "Deutschlandvertrag", which intended an automatic tie of the whole of Germany later to the "west treaties" of the Federal Republic of Germany. Also the SPD attacked the West German government and the west powers, because the (West German) Social Democrats wanted to make the reunification conditional on the west-integration of the whole of Germany. Therefore they had also demanded negotiations about the Soviet proposals before the conclusion of the "Deutschlandvertrag". Schumacher, the chairman of the SPD, had also hurled the following words at Adenauer during a session of the parliament: "Wer diesen Vertrag unterschreibt, hört auf, ein guter Deutscher zu sein!" (Who signs this treaty is coming to the end to be a good German)

A deputy of the FDP (Free Liberal Party of West Germany) made the analysis with the greatest extent. The western defence would have a defensive orientation, but the reunification would be formulated as offensive goal. Also it would be absurd to think, there is the possibility to "elect the Soviet Union out of Germany" by a free polling. The negotiations had to start with the question "what does a European security system look like to protect Germany enough and the Soviet Union doesn't consider as threat?" The west powers reacted with delaying tactics to the Soviet note of 10 March and demanded free elections as condition for negotiations about a peace treaty. The Soviet reaction followed on the heels of the conclusion of the "Deutschlandvertrag" and the treaty about the "European Defensive Community". The border between the German Democratic Republic and West Germany was blocked off, it was announced to set up an own army of the DDR and it was cleared the way for the forming of the socialism of the "**D**eutsche **D**emokratische **R**epublik" (**DDR/GDR** = **G**erman **D**emocratic **R**epublic).

We write the year **1953**

On 5 March died Stalin, the Soviet dictator, in Moscow. After his death the leading politicians of the Soviet Union thought an agreement with the west powers by concessions in the issue of Germany over. The Soviet occupying power in Germany arranged an extensive programme of liberalizing early in June in the DDR/GDR, to remedy the lacking credibility of its "Germany policy" so far. But the leadership of party and state of the DDR half-heartedly and unwillingly realized the Soviet arrangement only. So the raising of norms (the norm was the figure of work, which a labourer had to reach within an hour or day; each work was divided into figures, which were set by the state) for construction workers by 10% belonged to the half measures. A strike of the construction workers developed from a demonstration against the raising of the norms in East Berlin; this strike changed suddenly into a revolt against the political system of the DDR on 17 June. Within some hours spread this revolt to all big towns of the DDR. This revolt characterized destruction of part offices, attacks against party officials (SED) and finally the freeing of political prisoners. The commander-in-chief of the Soviet troops in the DDR declared the state of emergency, put into action executives and used the right of war, let drive tanks through the streets and let carry out mass arrests. After some hours broke the revolt down, only in the uranium mines of Saxony were the revolt and the demonstrations still lasting some days. Young persons, who threw stones at the tanks, demonstrated the helplessness of the whole of this operation. Thus nobody could eliminate the political system of the DDR, much less drive the Soviet Union out of its occupying zone (DDR/GDR). 18 demonstrators were sentenced to death by Soviet military courts and executed. Courts of the DDR sentenced to death 3 demonstrators and 1,383 to prison sentence. The West Germans could do nothing against these terrible occurrences in the middle of Germany, but they declared the June 17 as national holiday of West Germany.

The inactivity and helplessness in the west showed that the Americans neither disposed of a real concept for the roll back of the communism nor were willing to start a policy of understanding with the Soviet Union. John Foster Dulles, the new American Secretary of State (1953 – 1959), had refused the initiative of the re-elected British Prime Minister Churchill to hold a summit conference of the super powers in the spring time. The ratification of the treaty about the "European Defensive Community" had the absolute priority to the Americans. The (West-) German chancellor Adenauer settled on the American course. The axis Washington - Bonn became the determinant element of the politics within the western alliance in the years from 1953 to 1958. Adenauer's travel to the U.S.A. in April of this year became a procession of triumph. The Americans showed the Germans how they appreciate them as new partner of the west alliance.

The electoral battle in West Germany of this year was aimed at Konrad Adenauer as West-German chancellor by his party, the **CDU** (**C**hristian **D**emocratic **U**nion) according to the American example. The SPD and its (new) chairman Ollenhauer couldn't set something against Adenauer. The SPD had even to put up with the reproach to be communistically infiltrated and politically unreliable. Some publicists, amongst them Gustav Heinemann (he became West-German president later), fought in vain against the view, the Federal Republic of Germany (West Germany) could force the Soviet Union to abandon the DDR by a rearmament.

The election of September 6 became a great success to the West German chancellor. The success was also assessed all over as confirmation of his politics. 12,400,000 West Germans voted for the CDU/CSU (= 45.2%) - 7,900,000 voted for the SPD (=28.8%) – 2,600,000 voted for the FDP (the Liberals, = 9.5%) and for the party of the fugitives, the **BHE** (**B**und der **HE**imatvertriebenen), voted 1,600,000 West Germans (= 5.9%). The other parties failed because of the 5%-barrier. This barrier was a clause of the new (West-) German law. According to this clause each party has to reach at least 5% of the votes in the end of the polling to take really a seat in parliament. The result of the election was also read as a mark of political maturity of the new West German state and as a turning away from the splitting up of the parliament by too many parties in the period of the "Weimarer Republik/Weimar Republic" ("Bonn is not Weimar!").

Adenauer formed a coalition of all middle-class parties of West Germany after the election. This coalition had a two thirds majority in the West German parliament (Bundestag).

We write the year **1954**

In January and February sat in conference the foreign ministers of the four powers in Berlin; this conference replaced the summit meeting that Churchill had suggested. The American strategy during this conference was, to reveal the impossibility of an agreement with the Soviet Union in a propagandist and effective way. The Americans did this to put France under pressure in order to ratify finally the treaty about the "**EVG**" (**E**uropäische **V**erteidigungs**G**emeinschaft/European Defensive Community). But the decision on the "EVG" wasn't made in Berlin; the decision was made far away from Berlin, in Indochina (Vietnam, Cambodia, Laos) On 7 May surrendered the French soldiers of the jungle fortress Dien Bien Phu in the French colony Indochina. The French soldiers combated the rebels of Viet-Minh, a liberation movement. The defeat of Dien Bien Phu was the reason for the resignation of the French government now. The French government under Mendes-France (1954 – 1955) liquidated immediately three operations: the war in Indochina, the colonial war in Tunisia and the treaty about the "EVG" (EDC = European Defensive Community). On 30 August the French "National Assembly" (parliament) also rejected the treaty about the "EVG". So the creation of a "European Defensive Community" failed because of the French rejection of the treaty about this organization.

The 30 August was the darkest day of Adenauer as West German chancellor. But a few months later could get drawn up another solution by way of compensation, the admission of the Federal Republic of Germany into the **NATO** (**N**orth **A**tlantic **T**reaty Organization). That happened by means of British arrangement. In the protocol to the admission West Germany declared against the disposal of nuclear weapons. At the same time made Bonn and Paris a treaty about Saarland "to be a European state". Both treaties (the admission into the NATO and the treaty about Saarland) were signed by West Germany on 23 October in Paris; therefore they were also called the "Treaties of Paris". The "Treaties of Paris" led also to the end of the occupying regime of the west powers in West Germany and to the foundation of the "West European Union". On 25 October was publicized the French-German agreement on Saarland; Saarland "should be never again a part of Germany" (but that was to be changing some time later). It's true that the opposition of the SPD to the "Treaties of Paris" was lasting, but the members of the leadership of this party also said that they are willing to change the course, if there would break down new negotiations between the west powers and the Soviet Union about the reunification of Germany.

On 12 November refused the FDP (the liberal party of West Germany), the coalition partner of the CDU, to agree to the treaty of 23 October about Saarland, which was also really a provisional treaty only, therefore the FDP demanded to continue the negotiations about this problem now.

In this year took place the world cup (football -- in U.S.A. and Australia: soccer) in Bern, the capital of Switzerland. West Germany reached the final and had Hungary as opponent. In the preliminary round Hungary had won the football/soccer match against West Germany by goals 8 to 3. After 8 minutes of the final the Hungarians had already scored two goals against West Germany. Now the German football (soccer) players fought hard and reached that, what seemed to be impossible. The final result was three goals for West Germany to two goals for Hungary.

West Germany was the first time world cup winner, world champion. The whole of Germany was in a flap. Germany was an important state to the world again, caused by the "Wunder von Bern" (Miracle of Bern). The people of the western part of Germany celebrated this miracle for day and days.

In 1954 Konrad Adenauer was in Washington, United States. With President Dwight D. Eisenhower he had some talks.

Dwight D. Eisenhower   **Konrad Adenauer**

The last German prisoners of war are back

Two German armies

The European Economy Community

We write the year **1955**

On 5 May had all states, which had taken part in the conference of Paris, ratified the "Treaties of Paris" and West Germany became a sovereign state. The answer of the Soviet Union followed on the heels by the conclusion of an alliance with the communistic East European states, amongst them the **DDR** (Deutsche Demokratische Republik/**GDR** = German Democratic Republic). The treaties were made in Warsaw/Poland, therefore also the name "Treaty of Warsaw". The Soviet Union showed at the same time its consent to the détente by the agreement to the treaty with Austria. Austria became an independent state with self-chosen neutrality in May of this year. Until May Austria was occupied by the four super powers, United States, Great Britain, France and the Soviet Union. Austria committed itself also to aim never again at a reunification with Germany. Whilst Austria declared its neutrality West Germany was admitted into the NATO (North Atlantic Treaty Organization) on 9 May. The agreement with Austria was considered to be a good signal for the summit conference of the four super powers to which the west powers had invited immediately the Soviet Union after the ratification of the "Treaty of Paris". Topic of the talks of the four super powers during the summit conference was: reunification of Germany, the European security and the disarmament. The delegations of the super powers were sitting in conference between 17 and 23 July in Geneva/Switzerland. Sir Anthony Eden, the new Prime Minister of Great Britain (1955 – 1957) and successor of Churchill, presented a plan, which bears his name, of reunification of Germany by free election to the participants of the conference. The answer of the new Soviet president, Nikolai A. Bulganin (1955-1958), was a burial singing on the German unity. A "mechanical reunification" at the expense of the "social achievement" of the GDR couldn't be any more possible after the admission of the "Federal Republic of Germany" into the NATO. The conference was of use to the Soviet Union for the publicity of its politics of peaceful coexistence on the basis of the existent relations. The contrary proposals were summarized in a formula of compromise. The "Spirit of Geneva" led thus to the decline of the "cold war" in spite of lacking concrete results.

The Germans were very disappointed at the result of the conference. Now they pinned their hopes on the invitation of the Soviet Union to the (West) German chancellor, Konrad Adenauer, to come to Moscow. In September thus Adenauer went to Moscow. There the Soviet Union offered a new beginning of the relations between the Soviet Union and the Federal Republic of Germany and suggested the establishing of diplomatic relations to West Germany. Adenauer ignored the objection of the majority of his assistants and said "yes". He obtained in return for it the word for the release of the last German prisoners of war (more than 10,000 German soldiers were still in Soviet captivity since the last war). The German population thought highly of Adenauer for the release of the last German prisoners of war, because it was a human feat of Adenauer for the Germans.

There were two German embassies in Moscow, which also said that there were two German states for ever. Bonn formulated the "Hallstein-Doctrine" to rule out these consequences. Prof. Walter Hallstein was lawyer, diplomat and leader of the German delegation during the negotiations about the "Schuman-Plan" (Montan Union) 1950 in Paris. He was permanent secretary in the Kanzleramt (office of chancellor) in the year of 1950/51 and in the years 1959 till 1967 first president of the commission of the "European Economy Community" (EEC). In the year of 1955 he programmed the foreign politics of West Germany; according to the programme West Germany should be entitled alone to keep up diplomatic relations with other states. That was the so-called "Hallstein-Doctrine".

A little piece of reunification could West Germany obtain more or less unintentionally. A decision by plebiscite about the acceptance of the "European Statute" was worked into the "Treaty of Saarland" (Saarvertrag) at France's request. On 23 October voted the inhabitants of Saarland with two thirds majority against this statute. France respected the result of the plebiscite and agreed to the annexation to the "Federal Republic of Germany". The date for the annexation should be the 1 January 1957.

This year were also started the great discussions about the statute of the future West German army. All parties of the West German parliament (Bundestag) were agreed that the new army can't possibly develop again into "a state in a state" and must be under supervision of the "Bundestag" (parliament). The structure of the West German army should be formed according to the principles of the "innere Führung" (Interior leadership of the army, which had already formulated the Reform's General Wolf Graf von Baudissin in the year of 1907: The soldiers must be educated to be willing and capable of defending freedom and right (citizen in uniform). The universal compulsory military service should be the basis of the army with a maximum of 500,000 soldiers. – The planning of the years 1950 – 1952 was determined by the aim, to activate a mass army in a short time. But in the meantime the military strategy of the west powers had changed decisively.

We write the year **1956**

On 1 January were the first voluntary soldiers called up. The United States and Great Britain began with the reduction of their land forces in favour of the nuclear armament simultaneously.

On 18 January decided the government of the DDR also to build up an own army, the "**N**ationale **V**olks**A**rmee" (**NVA**/National People's Army). The first Minister of Defence of the DDR/GDR became Willi Stoph, who was also Vice-Minister President of the DDR. Then on 28 January was the army of the "**G**erman **D**emocratic **R**epublic" (**GDR**) admitted to the "Pact of Warsaw", what was the easterly counterpart of the NATO. The admission happened during the "Conference of Warsaw".

On 8 February was decided in West Germany, to introduce the universal compulsory military service. Each soldier had to service in the army 18 months now. The law on the universal compulsory military service was passed by the West German parliament (Bundestag) on 6 July.

On 17 August was the KPD (Communistic Party of West Germany) declared illegal by the uppermost West German court of justice, the "Bundesverfassungsgericht" in Karlsruhe (Federal Constitutional Court in Karlsruhe/city in the country Baden-Württemberg). The communists were declared enemies of the democracy, enemies of West Germany.

On 25 September visited Adenauer Belgium. There he met with a friendly reception in the palace of Laken. Topic of conversation with the Belgian king Baudouin was amongst other things the treaty about the correction of the German-Belgian frontier, which was concluded by both states one day ago. The correction of the year of 1949 was cancelled with it.

There was also a revolution in October of this year in Hungary. The Hungarians revolted against the Soviet occupying troops and against the communistic system in the own country. The rebellions were bloodily put down by the Russian troops. It was a catastrophe for Hungary, but also for Europe. Hungary's dream of an own free country was brought to an abrupt end for many years. Many Hungarians were executed and many fled to Austria and West Germany.

The year
1956, a
fateful
year, but
a year of
certainty
too

More than 10 years she has been waiting, more than 10 years she has heard nothing from him, more than 10 years, she has never give up hope, more than 10 years have passed, after more than 10 years now, a message and the certainty: He's never coming back, he died in Siberia, far away from home; he died in captivity in the Asian part of Russia where he has suffered more than 10 years, suffered for a senseless war which he had not wanted, which was the war of a madman, a man who wanted to rule over the world, so began a war that brought only suffering to millions, a war in which several million people had to die too.

We write the year **1957**

Saarland became officially a part of (West-) Germany. It was a country of the Federal Republic of Germany now. Adenauer made a trip into this country after the reunion with (West-) Germany. There he was met with an enthusiastic reception. The inhabitants of Saarland cheered, they were Germans again, Germans according to their sentiment.

This year was to become a great year to Germany and Europe. The states of the "Montan Union" had their last and greatest success in the European politics. On 25 March were made the treaties about the establishment of the "Europäische WirtschaftsGemeinschaft" (**EWG**/ European Economic Community = **EEC**); these treaties, which were signed in Rome, therefore also called "The Treaties of Rome", became effective then on 1 January 1958. The 25th of March was thus the "day of birth of the **European Union**", as this organization was called later. The states of the hour of the birth were: West Germany, France, Italy, Belgium, the Netherlands and Luxembourg. The EWG/EEC got new sales chances for the West German export industry. But the West German farming had to prepare itself for a hard competition. 1955 was still promised an intensified support of the West German farmers by means of the "Grüne Pläne" (Green Plans). Many farmers couldn't stand the competition and had to give up their farms. But the Social Democrats stopped their resistance to the politics of integration and agreed to the "Treaties of Rome".

Adenauer had already decided in the year of 1955 to win the parliamentary elections to the "Bundestag" (Lower House of the West German parliament) by means of internal successes. Motto of his party (CDU) should be the reform of the social insurance. Basic idea of the reform of pension was that nobody could assume that the long-standing principle of accumulation of capital would be safe also in future, because the capital had been used up by inflation and war. The money for the pensions had to get raised by the working population; only the continuously increasing wages and thus also the increasing insurance contributions permitted to pay higher pensions. Adenauer got through against the intention of his minister for economic affairs and against his minister of finance that the reform of pension provides a periodical adjustment of the pensions to the development of the gross wages. Also the Social Democrats voted for the law on the reform of the pensions, which was passed in January of this year.

The intensified promotion for houses of one's own within the scope of the social house building led to the integration of the petty bourgeois classes. The rebuilding, the increase of wages, the beginning cut of the working week and also the motorizing wave led at the voters to a mood of contentment with the present conditions. This mood was also touched on by the slogans of the CDU/CSU during the electoral battle of this year now.

Friendly election posters with the portrait of the chancellor and his minister for economic affairs (Prof. Ludwig Erhard) claimed: "Keine Experimente" (No experiments) and promised: "Wohlstand für alle" (prosperity for everybody). The leading candidates of the SPD were rather unconvincing in comparison with the mottoes of the CDU/CSU; also the posters and the electoral agitation of the SPD had no effect on the voters. On 6 September achieved Adenauer a great election victory, which was more radiant than the victory of the year of 1953. 15,000,000 West Germans cast their vote for the CDU/CSU (= 50.2 %) – 9,500,000 West Germans cast their vote for the SPD (= 31.8 %) – 2,300,000 West Germans cast their vote for the FDP (= 7.7 %) –

1,400,000 West Germans cast their vote for the BHE (= 4.6 %) and 1,000,000 West Germans cast their vote for the DP (= 3.4 %). It was the first time in the German history that a party had reached the absolute majority in the parliament.

The great internal success of Adenauer coincided with a visible change of the military power proportions. On 4 October launched the Soviet Union the first satellite. It was the "Sputnik" that revolved round the Earth now. By it demonstrated the Soviet Union the stage of development of its rocket technique too. The United States were within the range of Soviet intercontinental ballistic missiles now. The coupling of the Federal Republic of Germany to the military super power U.S.A. served for the security of the West, but it wasn't a starting point for the reunification.

In this year was the equipment of the West German army with nuclear weapons going to be a special issue: "Die taktischen Waffen sind nichts weiter als die Weiterentwicklung der Artillerie" (The tactical/nuclear weapons are nothing else as the further development of the artillery). In April of this year Adenauer had interfered in the public debate (that it was in the meantime) for the nuclear equipment of the West German army with these words, which played the problem down. He gave rise to a flood of protests by it. The "Manifesto of Göttingen" on 12 April formed the preliminary stage to the "Kampf-dem-Atomtod"-movement (battle-against-the-nuclear-death-movement), what preoccupied the West German population in the following two years. In the "Manifesto" claimed 18 prominent atomic physicists, amongst them Otto Hahn, Werner Heisenberg and Carl Friedrich von Weizsäcker, West Germany's voluntary renunciation of nuclear weapons as contribution to the securing of the world peace and stated publically their refusal to cooperate in the manufacture and tests of nuclear weapons. The appeal of the scientists met with a positive response in the greatest part of the public of West Germany (so in Churches, Labour Unions and many cities), but without to give already rise to the appearance of a peace movement in the streets and squares of the West German cities. – In December, the NATO decided to store American nuclear weapons on the soil of West Germany.

We write the year **1958**

On January 23 Adenauer listened to the words of Thomas Dehler, a member of the party FDP, and Gustav Heinemann, who had gone over to the SPD in the meantime, during a night session. Both settled up with Adenauer during this session and reproached him for his failed "Germany-policy". The absolute majority of CDU/CSU and **DP** (**D**eutschland **P**artei) voted for a motion on March 25, which in an encoded form authorized the West German government to equip the West German army with nuclear weapons. That happened after the following foreign debate between 20 and 25 March in the parliament (Bundestag). This resolution gave a massive impetus to the peace movement. On March 22 appeared the action group "Kampf-dem-Atomtod" already before the public. This group was especially supported by the SPD and **DGB** (**D**eutscher **G**ewerkschafts**B**und/German Federation of Labour Unions). The action group "Kampf-dem-Atomtod" pointed to the danger by the nuclear armament and claimed a public opinion poll on the problems of the nuclear equipping of the West German army. Everybody in West Germany could see the placards of the group "Battle-against-the-Nuclear-Death" (Kampf-dem-Atomtod) in the cities and villages.

There were protest vigils in some cities and during a big demonstration were more than 200,000 people up and about in April of this year. In some cities there were spontaneous strikes in the course of the extra-parliamentary action of "Kampf-dem-Atomtod"-movement. Calls for a "political strike" to prevent a nuclear armament could everybody hear sporadically during the demonstrations, but by these calls were the leadership of the SPD and the labour unions in a bad trouble.

It is true that the prohibition of the public opinion poll by the "Bundesverfassungsgericht" (Constitutional Court of West Germany), what happened on July 30, sealed the soon decline of the "Kampf-dem-Atomtod"-initiative, but it doesn't mean the final out of this "armament-critical" movement within the Federal Republic of Germany. On "Good Friday" of this year came so into being the idea of the "Easter Marches" in Great Britain. That happened under the responsibility of the philosopher Bertrand Russell. With beginning of the sixties was the "Easter March"-movement, which was a traditional movement in the meantime, also called into being in West Germany.

The further development of the diplomatic relations between the Federal Republic of Germany and the Soviet Union was undecided since 1955, the year of the beginning of the relations. The visit of the Soviet Vice-Prime Minister, Anastas Mikoyan, in April in Bonn stood for a chance for an understanding to the following ten years. Chancellor Adenauer had given up the hope of a reunification by means of the policy of strength in the meantime and wanted to negotiate about the change of the DDR into a neutral state like Austria. But the DDR wasn't any more at Soviets' disposal. Thus perhaps could only be planned negotiations about a peace treaty with the whole of Germany as long-term objective only. So remained the only possibility, to come to an agreement of a peaceful coexistence between both German states, to keep the frontier's affair open and thus also to prevent the partition of Germany for ever. West Germany's renunciation of nuclear weapons was the prerequisite for Mikoyan to further negotiations, he warned against the realization of the resolution of the West German parliament about the nuclear armament. Adenauer didn't comply with Mikoyan's wishes for West Germany's renunciation of nuclear weapons. Mikoyan's visit in Bonn came thus to an end without result. – On the other hand the Soviet Union was pestered by the DDR to take action against the position of the west powers in West Berlin. The existence of West Berlin as an island of the freedom and western way of life in the middle of the German Democratic Republic (DDR) hindered this communistic republic from its consolidation and did the DDR (GDR) a big economic harm by the refugees, who left continuously the GDR (DDR) via West Berlin, what was caused by the situation in the GDR. In November of this year took the Soviet Union the diplomatic offensive and terminated all existing agreements of the four powers on the status of the whole of Berlin by a note, time limit to the termination: six months. At the same time the Soviet Union suggested the creation of a demilitarized "Free City West Berlin" to the west powers. By a second note the Soviet Union suggested the conclusion of a peace treaty with both German states, which should also comprise the ban on nuclear weapons.

On 20 October visited the German president, Heuss, Great Britain and met with a friendly reception by the English Queen, Elisabeth II, there. Some days later was West Berlin in a flap, Bill Haley the great "Rock-'n'-Roll" star was in concert there. After his concert it came about tumults by young persons, quite a few were hurt during these tumults.

We write the year **1959**

The cautious reaction of the Americans and British to the Soviet Union note showed the changed military proportion of power of the last years. The United States had lost their superiority and hinted cautiously at their readiness to make the "Germany-political" items of the Federal Republic of Germany to the basis for negotiations. That should happen to secure the own position in Berlin. Adenauer was seeking in this situation for dependence on the French President "General de Gaulle", who had taken up his office one year ago. De Gaulle's foreign goal was the re-establishment of the French super power. That was a goal that France had always pursued. But to reach this goal needed France an own nuclear army. De Gaulle also needed the economic security by the Federal Republic of Germany (West Germany) for his arms policy, therefore he promised to fulfil the treaties about the "European Economic Community" (EEC). But he refused the political goal of the EEC (**E**uropäische **W**irtschafts**G**emeinschaft/**EWG**), the integration of Europe. This constellation led to the alliance between Paris and Bonn and determined the last phase of Adenauer's foreign politics in the years between 1958 and 1963.

On 1 January of this year came also into force the treaty about the "European Economic Community". This treaty was concluded on 25 March, 1957 in Rome, as we know. In the states of the community, in France, Italy, Belgium, the Netherlands, Luxembourg and West Germany, was especially celebrated this day now. Is this community perhaps a Union already? No, this became realty later, a union together with other European states.

In this year (on September 12) expired the term of office of the first President of West Germany, Theodor Heuss. On 7 April Konrad Adenauer surprisingly announced his candidacy for president of the Federal Republic of Germany, the highest state post in West Germany. By it he wanted to become the successor of

Theodor Heuss. But on 4 June he renounced again this post. His reason was the present complicated foreign situation. On June 15 became new candidate for the highest state post Heinrich Lübke, who was minister of agriculture and member of the CDU.

On 18 June became "Schloß Bellevue" in West Berlin seat of the President of the Federal Republic of Germany although West Berlin didn't belong to this West German republic. Thus was the West German president also present in West Berlin, what was tolerated by the west powers. West Germany wanted to demonstrate by it that the President of the Federal Republic of Germany has jurisdiction also over the inhabitants of West Berlin.

On 1 July was Heinrich Lübke elected President of the Federal Republic of Germany **in West Berlin**. The first congratulator was Konrad Adenauer.

On 27 August visited the first time an U.S.-American president the Federal Republic of Germany (West Germany). It was Dwight D. Eisenhower. He had some important talks with the West German government in Bonn, the capital of the Federal Republic of Germany. Topic of the talks was the general situation in West Germany and Europe. West Germany showed itself as close friend of the United States during this visit.

On 12 September the West German president, Theodor Heuss, handed over the official duties to his successor in office, Heinrich Lübke. Heinrich Lübke was to become a colourless president, without charisma, contrary to Theodor Heuss, who was called "Father of the nation" (Papa Heuss).

There was a political incident on 6 October in West Berlin. "S-Bahn" stations in West Berlin, which were maintained by the

DDR, were provided with national emblems of this communistic state. The S-Bahn, which was a speed tram through the whole of Berlin, belonged to the German Democratic Republic, but in spite of that were the stations in West Berlin no territorial ground of this state. Now there were clashes with the police of West Berlin, because the policemen removed again the national flags of the DDR. These clashes were to be no the only clashes in future.

On 20 November was founded the **European Free Trade A**ssocia-tion (**EFTA**) in Stockholm/Sweden. This association should be-come the counterpart of the **EWG** (**E**uropäische **W**irtschafts**G**ermeinschaft = **E**uropean **E**conomic **C**ommuni-ty/**EEC**) It is true that the EFTA was existent many years, but this association reached never the importance of the EWH/EEC. Therefore this association was also liquidated later. Another reason for the liquidation was that many states of the EFTA joined the European Union (the succeeding organization of the EWG/EEC). The founder members of the EFTA were the follow-ing states:

Austria, Denmark, Norway, Sweden, Switzerland, Portugal and Great Britain.

On 21 December came the summit conference of the three west powers to an end in Paris. The three west powers confirmed the defence of West Berlin and made simultaneously the Soviet Un-ion an offer of disarmament talks, which should take place on March 15 of the following year in Geneva/Switzerland. The Sovi-et Union promised to come to Geneva.

The catastrophe of Hamburg

The construction of the Berlin Wall and the death zone between West and East Germany

"Ich bin ein Berliner"

We write the year **1960**

Also in the DDR/GDR grew stronger the political economy in the year of 1957, so that on 28 May 1958 the food cards (as we know, everybody could get essential foods only in return for a special food card) could be abolished for ever. Till 1961 the German **D**emocratic **R**epublic (**GDR**/DDR) should have caught up the **F**ederal **R**epublic of **G**ermany (**FRG**/West Germany) with the production and consumption of foodstuffs and consumer goods. The "Zehn Gebote der sozialistischen Moral" (ten rules of the socialist moral), which were promulgated by Walter Ulbricht, should help to reach this aim. Another way to reach this aim should be the multiplied establishment of "**L**andwirtschaftliche **P**roduktions**G**enossenschaften" (**LPG**'s/Agricultural Production Cooperatives). The collectivizing of the GDR-agriculture had been done, often pressed ahead with brutal means, on 15 April of this year. Many farmers had fled to West Germany. At the same time was also forced the merger of the manual worker's enterprises into "**P**roduktions**G**enossenschaften des **H**andwerks" (**PGH**/Production Cooperatives of the Manual Workers). The mass exodus of the farmers concerned had an effect, the second "Five-Year-Plan" was replaced by a "Seven-Year-Plan" with numbers for the annual production aim, which were kept down now (the numbers were substantially lower than before !).

On March 12 the West German chancellor, Konrad Adenauer, started a journey to the United States and Japan. In the U.S.A. he had political talks with the secretary-general of the UNO, Dag Hammarskjöld, with the Israeli head of government, David Ben-Gurion, and the American President Eisenhower. In Tokyo/Japan talks about the economic cooperation between the EWG (EEC = European Economic Community) and Japan came to the fore.

Whilst Adenauer was travelling through the United States and Japan, the "Bundestag" (West German parliament) in Bonn decided to privatize the company "Volkswagen", which was in possession of the West German state. The state possession "Volkswagen" (VW) was changed into a "stock corporation". 60% of the capital stock was sold to private persons, 40% remained possession of the country Lower Saxony and the West German state.

On 31 March Adenauer gave a speech to the Japanese parliament (he was the first foreign head of government who gave a speech to the Japanese parliament), whilst the European parliament in Strasbourg passed the "Hallstein-Plan", which had aimed at an accelerated achieving of the "Common Market".

On 8 April was settled by the Netherlands and the Federal Republic of Germany the question of the German reparation and the regulation of the trade and the re-establishment of the prewar frontier between both states. The Netherlands gave back the places Elten and Selfkant to West Germany. Today both places belong to the country "North Rhine-Westphalia".

On 14 April was the collective agriculture realized by force in the GDR. By it lost the free farmers their possession there. Two weeks later the government of the GDR also prohibited the own inhabitants from using the word "Deutschland" (Germany) in maps and atlases; now it was only allowed to use the "new official" name "**D**eutsche **D**emokratische **R**epublik" (**DDR**/**G**erman Democratic Republic = **GDR**).

On 1 May the biggest rally of West Berlin's history took place. 750,000 persons demonstrated against the Soviet menaces.

On 8 September issued the GDR-government, one day after the death of the first president of the GDR (DDR), a decree about the permission to set foot on the territory of East Berlin only by means of a special paper. But that paper was only necessary for inhabitants of the Federal Republic of Germany (West Germany), they had also to specify, why they want to set foot on the territory of the capital of the German Democratic Republic, because it was only allowed to visit relatives there. The West German government terminated the trade agreement with the GDR now; that was the reaction of West Germany to the decree of the GDR (DDR). But on 30 December both German states signed a new agreement again.

Another event in the GDR of this year:

After the death of Wilhelm Pieck, the first president of the "**G**erman **D**emocratic **R**epublic" (**GDR**/**D**eutsche **D**emokratische **R**epublik = **DDR**), was formed a "Staatsrat" (Council of State) instead of the president office up to now. That happened on September 12 of this year. Walter Ulbricht became "Staatsratsvorsitzender" (Chairman of the Council of State). On January 10 Walter Ulbricht was already elected chairman of the "Nationaler Verteidigungsrat" (National Defence Council) and thus appointed military commander-in-chief of the army of the GDR (East Germany; but it was really a German part in the middle of Germany, because Silesia, East Pomerania and East Prussia belonged still to Germany, officially till 1990!)

1960, the new generation, self-confident and industrious

After the war, another generation grew up that had expected a promising future. West Germany had become an economic power, respected by the world. Unfortunately that has not been told of the GDR, the Communist part of Germany.

We write the year **1961**

On 15 February the "**Vo**lks**po**lizei" (**Vopo**) of the GDR (people's police of the GDR) announced facilities in the allotment of compulsory permits to inhabitants of the Federal Republic of Germany who wished to visit their relatives in East Berlin. – In August began the army of the GDR to seal off the territory of its communist state. In the night between 12 and 13 August troops of the "Volksarmee" (people's army of the GDR) and the "Volkspolizei" surprisingly occupied the Soviet sector of Berlin and immediately started to seal off the territory of East Berlin by a barrier of barbed wire with a length of 45 km, which ran crosswise through Berlin. The army of East Germany ignored by the occupation of East Berlin the "Four-Power-Agreement". According to this agreement between the U.S.A., the Soviet Union, Great Britain and France it wasn't allowed that German troops set foot on the territory of Berlin; it didn't matter where in Berlin, in the east or in the west of this city. In the following months and years was the barrier completed little by little to a trough wall with ingenious safety equipment, which brought the free traffic between the east and west part of Berlin to an end for long; as we know, Berlin was divided into four sectors in the year of 1945, the three west sectors: the British, U.S.-American and French sector – and the east sector: the Russian sector. The east sector of the former German capital was controlled by the Soviets (Russians) and became an integrated part of the GDR. West Berlin (the three west sectors) was an isolated western enclave in the middle of the territory of the **G**erman **D**emocratic **R**epublic (**GDR**/DDR).

Aim of the blocking off (barrier) was, to make impossible the escape from East Berlin to West Berlin for the inhabitants of the GDR; the reason was the number of refugees, which had been on the increase. In the years between 1945 and 1961 3,200,000 inhabitants of the east zone (= Soviet zone, since 1949 German Democratic Republic) made off; they left this communist part of Germany and fled to West Germany. That caused economic problems because of the manpower shortage now there in the GDR. By the expansion of the barrier system (blocking off system of the GDR/DDR), which became hardly surmountable, went rapidly down the number of refugees. In the years between 1961 and 1968 succeeded only 27,000 East Germans in fleeing from the German Democratic Republic that never was a democratic state. More than 70 persons lost their life during the run to the West in the years between 1961 and 1968. They were victimized by the blocking off devices or were shot dead by East German soldiers.

The construction of the Berlin Wall had a far-reaching aftermath for the population of the divided city. Before the wall was constructed crossed more than 60,000 persons the demarcation line every day, to go about their work in the other part of Berlin - 50,000 persons of East Berlin did their job in West Berlin and 10,000 persons from the western part were working in East Berlin. 70% of the inhabitants of West Berlin had also relatives in East Berlin. Now were East and West Berlin hermetically sealed off from each other by the wall; the most of the 81 border crossing points were shut down; the remaining border crossing points, like Checkpoint Charlie that was a border crossing point only for foreigners or the crossing point Friedrichstraße, gave only the possibility to the traffic of passing very slowly these points. Inhabitants of West Berlin could go only to East Berlin, if they had a special allowance (a special paper, the so-called Passierschein/special permit) to set foot on the territory of the GDR. But the inhabitants of East Berlin didn't have the possibility to go to West Berlin, to visit their relatives there; the border was closed down for them. The only exception was, to have narrowly defined "urgent family affairs" or to be old-age pensioner, who could visit relatives in West Berlin or make once a journey into the Federal Republic of Germany every year since 1964. The construction of wall roused the people in the West to indignation; but this indignation they vented mainly by prohibited protests, because neither London, Washington and Paris nor the West German chancellor Adenauer wanted to risk an armed conflict with the Soviet Union. But now the governing mayor of West Berlin, Willy Brandt (he became West German chancellor later), demanded of the West Allies considerable steps, which were more concrete than the protests. Now the isolated city West Berlin got also a stronger assurance of protection by the west powers and reinforcement by American troops. The American Vice-President Lyndon B. Johnson visited West Berlin in this year, to confirm America's intent to defend this city against any attacks from the East. In the year of 1963 was to follow the American president John F. Kennedy.

On 22 October there was a burning situation at the checkpoints of Berlin. At the checkpoints of West Berlin appeared American tanks; by it the Americans wanted to demonstrate that they were prepared to defend this city against any aggressor. Some days later also appeared Soviet tanks on the eastern sides of the checkpoints. It threatened to break out a military conflict. The world peace was in danger for some years again.

On 22 November Chancellor Adenauer made a trip to the US. There he met the new American president John F. Kennedy to discuss with him the alarming situation in Germany. The most important topic of talk was the "Berlin affair". Kennedy assured Adenauer of the defence of West Berlin, if the Soviets would attack this part of the capital of the former German Empire. Kennedy also confirmed during the talk that the "Agreement of the four powers" on the whole of Berlin is still effective.

We write the year **1962**

In February occurred one of the biggest flood disasters of the German history. In the night between 16 and 17 February 40 million cubic metres water turned from the North Sea to a disastrous deluge in a suburb of Hamburg. Wilhelmsburg, a suburb of

Hamburg with a fifth of the municipal area of this Free City, was flooded. It was a catastrophe to the inhabitants of this seaport, 315 persons drowned in this night, 7,000 flats and 1,000 farms were destroyed, thousands and thousands of head of cattle drowned in the flood, the damage of property amounted to 870 million DM (= 440 million Euro)

Some days before the 16 February was already a weather situation brewing that let have a presentiment of the catastrophe of the night between 16 and 17 February. On 14 and 15 February was already a high-pressure area over the North Atlantic that extended from Spain to the Shetland Islands (Great Britain). At the same time a cyclone took form over the middle of Scandinavia. Between cyclone and the high-pressure area flowed cold air from the North Pole into the region of the North Sea. The growing storm got wind force 12 in gusts and thus hurricane force. The water mass was pressed through the mouth of the Elbe (river) against the Free City Hamburg and dammed up to a new high tide. On Friday, the 16 February, the waters had reached 2.4 m over middle-high tide in the afternoon. The water level didn't fall about 2.37 m as usual, because the storm was continuing with undiminished force. Now the water level was falling about 1.20 m only. It is true that the "Seewetteramt" (Sea Weather Office) continued to give running gale warning commentaries since this afternoon, but the inhabitants of Hamburg had got used to cellars, which were full of water and streets, which were flooded during a (normal) storm, so that nobody paid attention to this warning.

The competent authority of Hamburg sounded alarm after the message of the "Deutsche Hydrographische Institut" (Hydrographic Institute of Germany) that the coast of the North Sea and the area of the lower part of the Elbe will have a high tide of more than 3.0 m over middle-high tide (MHT/MHW = Mittelhochwasser) At 20:30 o'clock interrupted the North German Radio Station its programme the first time and it was read out the corresponding news. The television station announced the alarm at 22:15 o'clock; in the meantime was forecasted a high tide of 3.50 m over MHT (MHW). The people, who were living directly next to the dike, knew only the concrete danger, but in the Hanseatic City Hamburg, 100 km away from the sea, the people reckoned with wet feet only.

Now the danger became also clear to the competent authority of Hamburg; the responsible office gave alarm, degree III. The automatic water gauge in Cuxhaven (town nearer at the coast than Hamburg) broke down by a high tide of 3.20 m over **MHT** (Middle-High Tide). It was made preparations for the emergency. Dike federations, fire brigades, police, Technisches HilfsWerk (THW: a technical relief organization of Germany), the Red Cross and pioneering units of the Bundeswehr (West German army) were alerted, sandbags, boats and trucks were made available. But the civilian population wasn't especially warned, the evacuation was planned nowhere. In Wilhelmsburg, a suburb of Hamburg that was situated in a natural tub and surrounded of two branches of the Elbe was nobody worried.

At 1:00 o'clock in the night, we wrote already February 17, the water gauge broke down when reaching the height of 3.40 m over MHT. At 1:15 o'clock were inspected the first dikes in Hamburg-Wilhelmsburg. At 2:00 o'clock was measured once more the water height by expedients, there was 3.80 m over MHT. At 3:00 o'clock the dikes broke at more than 50 points – the catastrophe had begun. The garden colony of Wilhelmsburg, which was situated deeper than the centre of this suburb, was immediately washed away by the flood; then the flood wave had burst holes like craters into the streets of the centre and washed away motorcars and cut off escape routes. The people were fighting against the water mass into the morning, more than 300 persons drowned; the telephone connections were cut off in no time after the first water break-ins. The catastrophe area was isolated, the power connections were interrupted. It was emerging early in the morning that the suburb Wilhelmsburg was literally drowned overnight. The domestic senator of the "Free State Hamburg" at the time, Helmut Schmidt (he became chancellor of West Germany later), had taken care of the job to arrange a relief action. He organized the greatest duty in a disaster area of the Federal Republic of Germany so far; that happened by the action of 8,000 soldiers of the West German army, 4,000 soldiers of the NATO, 1,700 firemen, 2,000 men of the "Technisches Hilfswerk" (THW), more than 4,000 other helpers of various organizations and 5,000 policemen of Hamburg. These many helpers could rescue 1,130 persons from the direct danger of life, could 17,800 persons evacuate from the flooding area and could temporarily accommodate them. Also 6,000 persons could be supplied with food by boats and helicopters.

The flood catastrophe of Hamburg had shocked the people of West Germany, but the politics had to go on. So there was the West-East affair, which was the main thing to Germany at the moment. Adenauer was prepared to negotiate directly on human relief for the "Zone" (so the GDR was called in those days) with the Soviet leadership to prevent that Germany became an object of political settlements between the super powers. He was also willing to concessions. In June, during a talk with the Soviet ambassador Smirnov, he made a "burgfriede" (truce) and standstill agreement in the German affair. In the years of 1959/60 Adenauer's narrowest consultant, Hans Globke, already outlined a plan to buy the right of self-determination of the Germans from the Soviets by recognition of the "status quo" in Europe, but that limited in time for the present. But a concrete step wasn't taken along these lines.

On 14 October an American U-2-reconnaissance plane took pictures of Soviet missiles in Cuba, which were aimed at North America. The Soviets had already broken the American monopoly on atomic bombs in the year of 1949 and then in the year of 1953 the monopoly on hydrogen bombs. Four years later followed the launching of the first Soviet intercontinental ballistic missile. So the United States had been made nuclear-prone. Now, in the "Cuba Crisis" (caused, because the Soviets had deployed missiles on the island, which aimed at the U.S.A.), it seemed for a moment that a military collision of both atomic giants would be inevitable. But John F. Kennedy, the American President, could win his Soviet opponent Khrushchev to a diplomatic solution - even more - he had some talks about arms control on the basis of the territorial status quo with the Soviets. Both super powers agreed to mark and respect the mutual sphere of influence to answer by it the question of security – also in the middle of Europe!

This change from the "Cold War" to the "Détente" had taken the German politics unprepared to a great extent, particularly since the confrontation of the different systems in East and West continued undiminished in Berlin and along the "Zonengrenze" (border between West and East Germany). The West German government had a hard time with the change of foreign ideas, which were enforced as base of the West German democracy during the last ten years: Adenauer's original aim was, that is to say, to shift the weight of power in Europe and in the world by rearmament of (West) Germany and integration of the West German state into the West. He thought, someday that would only bring the reunification of Germany "in peace and freedom". Now it seemed that in the West nobody takes an interest in the German affair and the German problems; if the Federal Republic of Germany would have opposed the present situation and the new political development of those days it would have risked a political isolation.

We write the year **1963**

On 15 February West Germany broke the diplomatic relations to Cuba, because Cuba had recognized the DDR (GDR) as independent state. The same day was started the sixth party conference of the **SED** (**S**ozialistische **E**inheitspartei **D**eutschlands) in East Berlin, whilst the Soviet head of government was staying with the East German government there. During the party conference of the SED visited Nikita Khrushchev, the Soviet head of government, the Berlin Wall, which was also called "peace wall" in East Germany.

On 22 January signed Konrad Adenauer and the French president Charles de Gaulle a German-French good-will agreement, which designated a closer cooperation above all in foreign affairs. France rejected Great Britain's joining of the EWG (EEC) only some days later.

In April of this year announced the first chancellor of West Germany, Konrad Adenauer, he will resign his post after the recess in autumn. The reason for his decision was that more and more people, also within the own party, didn't agree to his politics. On 22 April was Ludwig Erhard named as his successor by the CDU/CSU.

The last days of June were great days for West Germany. On 23 June, it was a Sunday, set John F. Kennedy, the American President, foot on West Germany's ground. He landed at the airport Köln-Wahn (Cologne-Wahn). There he was met with a very friendly reception by the West German government and the population of the Rhineland. From there he went to Bonn, the capital of the Federal Republic of Germany, which was situated only some kilometres from the airport Köln-Wahn. Then, in Bonn, Kennedy had political talks about the situation in Germany and Europe with the West German government. On 26 June visited the American President West Berlin, there the "Governing Mayor", Willy Brandt, gave him a warm welcome. The inhabitants of West Berlin cheered enthusiastically him. Then, before the city hall of Schöneberg (district of West Berlin), he made a speech in front of 150,000 people. His historic words were: "All free people, wherever they may be living, are citizens of this city (West Berlin), therefore I'm proud as a free man to can say: **Ich bin ein Berliner**". After these words an enthusiastic burst of applause followed. Kennedy had won the hearts of the inhabitants of West Berlin. It was a great day for this city, but also a great day for the whole of Germany.

Two days after Kennedy's visit to West Berlin the head of the communist party and government of the Soviet Union, Nikita Khrushchev, visited East Berlin. The reason of his visit was the seventieth birthday of Walter Ulbricht, the head of government of the **G**erman **D**emocratic **R**epublic (**GDR**/DDR).

On 15 October resigned Adenauer his post as chancellor of West Germany; it happened after a time of government of 14 years. One day later was "Mr. Wirtschaftswunder" (Mr. Economic Miracle), Ludwig Erhard, elected chancellor of West Germany.

There was still a terrible murder this year. On 22 November visited John F. Kennedy, who was liked also by the Germans, the city Dallas in Texas. During the drive in open automobile with his wife Jacqueline and Governor John Connally and his wife Nellie, John F. Kennedy was shot dead by a sniper. The first and third shot hit him at throat and temple, the second shot hit governor Connally at the back. Jacqueline Kennedy climbed in panic from the back seat of the car towards a bodyguard. The governor survived the attempt on his life, but the American president died 25 minutes later in the "Parkland Hospital" of Dallas. The presumed culprit, Lee Harvey Oswald, was arrested short time later. Only two days later was also Oswald shot dead; it happened during the transfer to the prison of Dallas. The culprit was Jack Ruby, an owner of a night club, who was immediately arrested after the crime. On 25 November was John F. Kennedy buried, it happened in the presence of many heads of states, also the West German President was present at the burial. West Germany had lost a friend. Kennedy's successor became Vice-President Johnson.

On 12 December mourned also West Germany over an appreciated man, it was Theodor Heuss, the "Father of the Nation" (Papa Heuss, as he was called in Germany). He died at the age of 79 in Stuttgart (capital of the country Baden-Württemberg)

On 17 December came West Berlin and the DDR to an agreement, which gave inhabitants of West Berlin the possibility to visit their relatives in East Berlin between December 18 and January 5 of the following year. 1,250,000 inhabitants of West Berlin made use of this possibility now. The DDR (GDR) designated this agreement as "human concession".

Ludwig Erhard, Chancellor of the Federal Republic of Germany (West Germany) 1963 – 1966

Erhard was called "Mr. Wirtschaftswunder" (economic miracle), because he brought West Germany to economic prosperity.

We write the year **1964**

Under foreign minister Gerhard Schröder, who was member of the CDU and minister of the interior in the years of 1953 – 1961, were set up offices of commerce since the last year in Poland, Romania, Hungary and Bulgaria. This step wasn't connect with a diplomatic recognition, but it was a preliminary stage of the annulment of the "Hallstein-Doktrin"; these doctrines didn't give the possibility to have diplomatic relations to states that recognize also the **G**erman **D**emocratic **R**epublic (**GDR/DDR**), with the only exception of the Soviet Union. According to Schröder's idea should be the improvement of the relations to the East European states also effective as lever against the DDR. By the improvement of the diplomatic relations to the East European states expected Schröder an economic and political isolation of the East German rulers within the communist camp. But that wasn't the reality. The Soviets, who were alarmed by symptoms of disintegration within the "Pact/Alliance of Warsaw", gave the DDR backing. Thus it was impossible for West Germany to make east politics past Moscow or the leadership of the SED (Socialist United Party of East Germany).

On 12 June the "Staatschef" (head of state) of the DDR, Walter Ulbricht, and the Soviet head of government, Nikita Khrushchev, signed a "mutual assistance and friendship pact". The same day Chancellor Ludwig Erhard had talks with the American President Johnson. The result of these talks was that it was impossible to reach a reunification of Germany in the foreseeable future. West and East Germany had drifted too apart in the meantime.

In the sixties the holiday destination Italy was for many Germans. They were able to travel again, thanks to the German economic miracle.

On 5 October escaped 57 persons from East Berlin through self-dug tunnels to West Berlin. During the escape a refugee shot dead a non-commissioned officer of the army of the DDR. That caused again a political tension between West and East Germany. But the shooting death of a soldier of the East German army by a refugee was to be an exception, because from now were refugees shot dead by border soldiers of the DDR/GDR.

We write the year **1965**

On 20 January visited the West German chancellor, Ludwig Erhard, the French President Charles de Gaulle at the palace of Rambouillet close to Paris. During the political talks spoke de Gaulle against a (West) German participation in a NATO-atomic army. It turned out by it that Ludwig Erhard will have no success in the foreign politics in the future. It was thanks to him that he was more successful in the domestic politics than in the foreign politics. His popularity seemed to be unbroken. In this year he won more votes during the parliamentary elections to the "Bundestag" than Adenauer in the year of 1961. Erhard's party, the CDU, obtained together with the CSU of Bavaria 47.6% of the votes, the SPD 39.3% and the FDP (Liberals) 9.5%. Now Erhard announces during his policy statement that the post-war time would be over. He called upon the people to be moderate and sketched out the picture of a "formulized society", in which all interests and groups were combined without external pressure but by understanding. West Germany got really into difficulties one year later; it happened by the first noticeable recession after the last war.

We write the year **1966**

This year the growth rate of the gross national product dropped for the first time; one year later even below the zero limit. The unemployment figure rose on 2.1%, whilst there was a boom in the world. 700,000 – 800,000 persons were without job, which was a scandal in those days. The very cheap mineral oil entered into competition with the coal that produced a grave crisis in the industrial sector of the coal mining. The successes of the **NPD** (**Nationaldemokratische   Partei   Deutschlands/National-**

democratic Party of Germany) during the elections in the country Hessen were alarming. In autumn of this year took right-wing extremists, 7.9% had cast their vote for the NPD, their seats in Parliament of Hessen. Startled observers drew already parallels to the end of the first German democracy, the Republic of Weimar. But in fact was above all Erhard's fate at stake. He was left in the lurch by his own fellow-members of the party (CDU) one year after his personal election result; the "kleine Koalition" (small coalition = CDU/CSU + FDP) was crushed by the problem how the gap of cover in the budget of the state could get filled. There were missing 4,000,000,000 DM for the year 1967 (total amount of the budget: 74,000,000,000 DM). Now the main problem was: tax raise or not? It is true that the cabinet reached an agreement, but the parliamentary parties picked the trial of strength regardless of the chancellor, who looked lonely and apathetically on his fall. Mende, the chairman of the FDP, favoured a going together with the SPD after the resignation of the ministers of his party; but the Liberals (FDP) were unstable in the eyes of the SPD, therefore the Social Democrats rejected a connection with the FDP. The vice-chairman of the party SPD, Herbert Wehner, was in contact with Kurt Georg Kiesinger, who was Minister President of the country Baden-Württemberg. Kurt Georg Kiesinger was intended for the candidacy as chancellor by the parliamentary party of the CDU on 10 November. Then, on December 1, the majority of CDU/CSU and SPD elected Kiesinger new chancellor of West Germany. Ludwig Erhard had resigned his post before; he was forced by his own party to do that.

Kurt Georg Kiesinger, Chancellor of the Federal Repub-lic of Germany (West Germany) 1966 - 1969

It was already put out feelers for a possibility of a "great coali-tion" at the end of November of the year of 1962; it happened during the crisis of the government when the FDP forced the resignation of the Minister of Defence, Franz Josef Strauß (a Bavarian and member of the party CSU), who was incriminated by an affair (the "Spiegelaffäre"; Spiegel = a reputable magazine of West Germany). During those days failed the forming of a "great coalition" because of Adenauer's person, who rejected a coalition with the SPD. Now, four years later, seemed the wear and tear of power of the CDU/CSU to be so advanced after 17 years of government that the SPD hoped to distinguish itself as the better ruling party. The post as foreign minister and vice-chancellor took over the party leader of the SPD, Willy Brandt (the governing mayor of West Berlin). Herbert Wehner took his seat in cabinet as one of the 9 ministers of the SPD (CDU and CSU had together 10 minister's posts). With it had two former resistance fighters against the Nazis a post in a cabinet of the West German Republic. Both were denaturalized by the Nazis, now they were ministers in a cabinet, of which chancellor was a former member of the NSDAP (Nazi-Party). Also Franz Josef Strauß made a political comeback now. Also a former minister of the CDU, who had resigned from his post in protest against Adenauer's rearmament and had gone over to the SPD after failure of the party "**G**esamtdeutsche **V**olks**P**artei" (**GV**P), of which co-founder he was, belonged to the new government; it was the former minister of justice, Gustav Heinemann. The new government of West Germany was also called now: "Regierung der nationalen Versöhnung" (government of the national reconciliation)

Herbert Wehner

The suspicion that the unanimity also conjured up risks for the democracy, couldn't get redressed out of the parliament; especially critical citizens and many young persons had a suspicion of the unanimity. An opposition of only 50 persons in parliament could be never an effective counterweight to a government majority of 446 Members of Parliament. Now came really an "**Außer**Parlamentarische **O**pposition" (**APO** – extra-parliamentary opposition) into being, which soon took also antiparliamentary goals.

We write the year **1967**

The "great coalition" proved its legitimacy from the economic crisis, which – that thought many people – could be mastered commonly by both big parties only. The minister for economic affairs, Professor Karl Schiller (SPD) and the minister of finance, Josef Strauß (CSU), "performed their recipes harmoniously in front of the marvelling viewers", but that happened only for the time being. These recipes were due to the idea of a general control of the economy by the state. The state proved to be crisis helper without to infringe upon the market-economic rules. This happened by more orders, tax reduction and measures of help; all that gave the private side food for an investment incentive. The necessary money was raised by "deficit spending" according to the recipe of the English national economist John Maynard Keynes (1883 – 1946). By the "law of stabilization", which was put in force in this year, was made the necessary instrument. The representatives of the state, of the party to a wage agreement and of the science had a meeting – a meeting of the so-called "Konzertierte Aktion" (concerted action) – to carry through the measures without friction, if possible. There was also a question of the "social symmetry" during the arrangement of CDU/CSU and SPD – social symmetry was a neologism of Karl Schiller like the term "concerted action". "Social symmetry" meant to be socially well-balanced: the labour unions should be actually reserved in questions of new wage agreements to make possible that the companies could increase their profit and thus give them an incentive to investments. This concept came out even. The unemployment figure got astonishingly fast lower. Also in the Ruhr area (Ruhr-Pot) were the things looking up by bonus for the shutdown of unprofitable coal mines and the foundation of the "Ruhrkohle AG" (= stock corporation for coal in the region on the river Ruhr). Economic growth was, to all appearances, no longer a serious problem when only the crises management was right. The following ten years were to show, how illusive this hope was.

The **APO** (Auß**er**P**arlamentarische** **O**pposition/extra-parliamentary opposition) was particularly active this year. The appearance of this organization attributed to the missing great parliamentary opposition party and was – even if not exclusive – an expression of a conflict between the generations.

The APO started first as student's protest against the "full pro-fessor-university" and against the delay of a university reform, but it rapidly expanded into a fundamental revolt. The war in Vietnam and the poverty in the Third World, which made a mockery of the claim of the Western democracies to bring about a just world system, belonged to the contemporary-historic ex-perience of this revolt. The students gave vent to their anger during the state visit of the Iranian Shah Reza Pahlavi on June 2 in (West) Berlin. During the hard clashes of demonstrators with the police and Shah-loyal Iranians, who gave cheers for their ruler, was the student Benno Ohnesorg shot dead by a police-man. From now couldn't be stopped the protest rallies of the APO.

The month April of this year was also a sad month to West Germany. In the evening hours of April 25 docked a speedboat of the West German navy on the bank of the Rhine close to the cathedral of Cologne and took a colours-covered coffin on deck. The coffin contained the dead body of Konrad Adenauer, who died at the age of 92 on 19 April. There was fired a salute and a squadron of jet fighters flew over Cologne. By it was started the last journey of Konrad Adenauer upwards the Rhine in direction of Rhöndorf, Adenauer's place of residence. Statesmen of 54 nations had arrived to be present at the funeral obsequies amongst them were men, who normally steered clear of each other like General de Gaulle (France) and the American president Johnson. The old West German president Lübke laid the hands of both presidents into each other; then reconciling he laid his hands in the hands of the other presidents. One of the many pictures of the funeral obsequies, which went round the world: amongst the mourners was Ben-Gurion, Prime Minister of Israel 1948 – 1953 and 1955 – 1963, Adenauer's friend and partner of reconciliation with Israel.

The hard core of Adenauer's foreign activity was above all that he gave up making the traditional German seesaw policy between East and West. He did it in favour of the integration into the free West. But also he realized that peace and security for (West) Germany depended on an understanding with the East.

This year also happened a change in the political climate between West Germany and the East: the "Entspannung" (dé-tente). The government under Chancellor Erhard had already made up its mind about a gesture of détente, what happened under pressure of the Western Allies. In a "peace note" of March 24, 1966 was included a promise to exchange a formal non-aggression declaration with the East European states. But it was made no mention of the DDR. The Russian government in Moscow didn't even answer to the note. The great coalition professed itself to be for the policy of détente. It happened with its policy statement of April 12 of this year. The motto can be read as follows: "Menschliche Erleichterungen durch Annäherung beider deutscher Staaten" (human relief by rapprochement of both German states).

Egon Bahr moved under Foreign Minister Willy Brandt into the „Auswärtige Amt"(Foreign Office) as head of the planning staff whilst Willi Stoph, the head of the East German Council of Ministers, accepted an offer for negotiations of West Germany, but he demanded as condition the recognition of the DDR (German Democratic Republic) and West Germany's renunciation of claim to sole representation. The correspondence didn't cause concrete steps for the time being, in spite of that began a change of the political climate.

This year West Germany also entered diplomatic relations with Romania, one year later also with Yugoslavia. The diplomatic relations with Yugoslavia were broken off some years ago because of political differences. But East politics couldn't get done with these deviationists within the "Pact of Warsaw".

We write the year **1968**

In West Germany were the protests of the APO continued. On 11 April, it was a Maundy Thursday, was Rudi Dutschke, the spokesperson of the protest movement of the students, very seriously injured by several shots in Berlin. The assassin was an unskilled worker, 23 years old.

A chain of demonstrations, of riots and street battles seized the cities in West Germany during the following Easter days. Militant groups moved to the publishing houses of the combine of Axel Springer, they did it with fire sets, stones and other projectiles. The combine of Axel Springer had turned to an object of hate by its "making of opinion" (the newspaper "Bild"). The result of the Easter demonstrations: 400 injured persons and 2 dead men.

In this situation was Gustav Heinemann, the minister of justice, one of the few politicians who had the courage and also the possibility to work moderating on the rebellious youth. On 14 April, at the height of the Easter unrest, delivered Heinemann a short address on the radio and on television. He reasoned not only to the young demonstrators and demanded nonviolent demonstrations and a critical cooperation with the state, but also to the older generation. The social democracy tried above all in the period following to give the APO-movement a political home and to direct its impulses into the course of an extensive reformatory movement.

Another great incident of this year was the rebellion in Czechoslovakia. The rebellion there ought to be a peaceful rebellion against the communist rulers. The Czechs and Slovaks wished more freedom, whilst the communist states of Europe feared that Czechoslovakia could say goodbye to the communist alliance.

On 4 January the Czechoslovakian President Antonin Novotný had lost his office as secretary-general of the central committee of the Czech Communist Party. His successor became Alexander Dubček, a liberal man. This was the reason now that on 21 February was held a summit conference of the leaders of the communist parties of the Soviet Union, Poland, Hungary, Bulgaria, Romania, DDR(GDR) and Czechoslovakia in Prague. The goal of this meeting was the "stabilization of the continuity of the (communist) alliance" (Pact of Warsaw) between Czechoslovakia and the other communist states.

On 22 March Antonin Novotný also resigned his post as President of Czechoslovakia, as result the leaders of the communist parties of Bulgaria, Hungary, Poland, the Soviet Union and DDR had talks about the beginning liberalizing of the political life in Czechoslovakia (Spring of Prague). The next day started troops of the "Pact of Warsaw" off with manoeuvres at the frontier of Czechoslovakia. On 23 May travelled the Soviet Minister President Kosygin once more to Prague. On 25 May he left Prague again. He had tried in vain to prompt the leaders of the Czechoslovakian communist party to abandon their reformatory efforts. The gazette of the communist party of the Soviet Union (the Pravda) pointed the possibility out to the Czechoslovakian government on 11 July that its initiated reform of democratizing could lead to a situation like the year of 1956 in Hungary. Then between 13 and 15 July was held a summit conference of the leaders of the communist parties and governments of the Soviet Union, DDR, Bulgaria, Poland and Hungary in Warsaw, the capital of Poland. The politics of democratizing by Czechoslovakia was criticized with fierceness. On 12 August went Walter Ulbricht once more to Prague. There he met with an unfriendly reception. The Czechoslovakian government also remained very cool towards him.

Then on 21 August invaded troops from the Soviet Union, DDR (East Germany), Hungary and Bulgaria the Czechoslovakian state and gave the "Spring of Prague" an abrupt end. The invasion met with a passive resistance of the most people of Czechoslovakia; there were only some actions of resistance. But these actions caused also some wounded persons and some persons were even killed. The head of the communist party of Czechoslovakia, Alexander Dubček, the president of the "National Assembly", Josef Smrkovský, the Minister President, Oldřich Černik and Čestmír Císař, the chairman of the central committee, were taken to Moscow. Some days later was elected a new presiding committee during the secret meeting of the communist party in a factory by Prague. All reform politicians belonged to this committee. On 23 August then went many inhabitants of Prague on general strike that happened in protest against the invasion of foreign troops of the states of the "Pact of Warsaw". The same day travelled Ludvik Svoboda, the President of Czechoslovakia, to Moscow to negotiate with the Soviet government. On 26 August, after many talks with the Soviet government, the Czechoslovakians submitted to the pressure of the Soviet Union. This was the end of the reformatory policy. Now the leaders of the communist party of Czechoslovakia could go back to Prague together with President Svoboda. The rebellion of the Czechoslovakians against the communist system came thus to an end and the détente in Europe had suffered a serious setback. But the international situation of the politics changed rapidly. The Soviets hoped to get technological aid by the West to their new economic reform. Therefore they couldn't afford a conflict with the West, particularly since there were also hard combats between Russians and the Chinese on the Ussuri River.

In West Germany was the FDP for a political departure for East whilst the CDU/CSU gave up its position and had its origin in its former East policy to keep the German question open by a wait-and-see-policy.

We write the year 1969

On 5 May of this year convened the "Bundesversammlung" (= Federal Assembly of all Members of the West German Parliament and Representatives from all classes of the West German population to elect a new President. Members of the Parliament and Representatives are represented at this assembly with equal number) in Berlin to elect the successor of the second West German President Heinrich Lübke (The term of office of the German President amounts to 5 years. The President can be re-elected once only, thus is his total term of office not longer than 10 years). Heinrich Lübke, the simple and honest man from Sauerland (a region in North Rhine-Westphalia), was West Germany's representative in the world 10 years; he had pleaded West Germany's cause above all in the Third World. He likes also to travel there, because then he could make the worries and misery of the people of the Third World accessible to the (West) Germans. At the end of his term of office became Lübke, called his name as Nazi, in poor health and lonely, laughing-stock of many magazines. The attacks of the magazines applied to the state power, of which cause the President personified, but Lübke could set nothing against these attacks. Gustav Heinemann seemed in view of this authority's crisis to be the "man of the hour", therefore he became also candidate of the SPD for the highest office in West Germany. He was a man of the middle-class with an unemotional public appearance; he was also well received by the critical youth, an advocate of courage of his convictions and of rights of liberty. Also the FDP supported surprisingly the candidate of the SPD, who won the election with bare majority now. Gerhard Schröder (CDU), who was last Minister of Defence, was the loser of the presidential election. Heinemann spoke of a "transition of power". Since Friedrich Ebert (Republic of Weimar) was a Social Democrat head of state again.

The FDP, condemned itself to the political powerlessness as little opposition party, had got itself a progressive image and fetched critical intellectuals into its ranks under the new party leader Walter Scheel (since 1968). The conservative wing of the FDP kept still, at least as long as the consequences of this social-liberal course weren't evident: the governmental alliance with the SPD, which was traced out by the teamwork during the election of the "Bundesprädident" (President of the Federal Republic of Germany/West Germany), was not yet sealed. The "Bundes-tagswahl" (election to the Lower House of the West German parliament) of September 28 brought still a heavy defeat for the FDP then, whilst the SPD could win many votes. But also the CDU and CSU lost 1.5% of the votes, but together they remained nevertheless the strongest party, therefore was also Kurt Georg Kiesinger ready again for negotiations to a coalition with the SPD. But he was waiting in vain for a step of the SPD in this direction. On October 21 the "Bundestag" elected with SPD-FDP majority Willy Brandt as fourth chancellor of the Federal Republic of Germany. Vice-chancellor and foreign minister became Walter Scheel.

Brandt's predecessor Georg Kiesinger, who was a typical Swabian and characterized as "wandelnder Vermittlungsausschuss" (changing Mediation's Committee) because of his civilized dealing with the power, had played the part as "Landesvater" (father of the country) with pleasure also in Bonn, the capital of West Germany, during his term of office there (Kurt Georg Kiesinger was Minister President of the country Baden-Württemberg in the years between 1958 and 1966). Willy Brandt, the new chancellor, was of other stamp, made of sterner stuff. He bound to his person the hopes of the people how hardly another statesman, but he offended also many people, above all the adversaries who quarrelled with his part: he was born on December 18, 1913 as child of a saleslady in Lübeck (town in the country Schleswig-Holstein/North Germany). He went over to the "fighting Lefts of Weimar" as member of the "Sozialistischen Arbeiterpartei" (Socialist Party of the Labourers), which was a splinter group of the SPD. When Hitler conquered the power he emigrated to Norway; there he continued to fight against the Nazis. He went already back to Germany in the year of 1945, a country of ruins in those days. His real name was Herbert Karl Frahm, but now he became naturalized again under his new name Willy Brandt, what was his name as author. He became Member of Parliament, then "governing mayor of (West) Berlin" (1957 – 1966) and was since 1964 party leader of the SPD. When now the SPD supplied the head of government after 39 years (last SPD-chancellor was Hermann Müller, 1928 – 1930), so was it also a chapter of coming to terms with the past. By it, so was Brandt's opinion, had Hitler finally lost the war.

The slogan, under which the new ruling coalition from SPD and FDP tackled its governmental job, meant: "Risk more democracy". New forms of citizens' attendance (at the political life) and of political planning, legislative works that showed the political way and an extensive renewal of the institutes should especially strengthen the confidence of the critical youth in the democracy, so reforms in all sectors, thus also in the working sector.

When now Willy Brandt and Walter Scheel took the government over, was there for the first time the talk about "two German states". The turning away from Adenauer's conception of a "Politik der Stärke" (policy of strength) and his "non-recognition of the DDR" couldn't be clearer formulated. But recognition of the DDR relating to international law was also out of the question to Willy Brandt. His opinion was, it is possible that there were two German states but both are among one another no foreign states. He made therefore the DDR the offer of negotiations to avoid the continuation of the drifting apart of both German states. He wanted to negotiate especially about the question of a "togetherness" that should lead off from the settled coexistence.

Willy Brandt, German Chancellor 1969-1974

Terrorism in West Germany

We write the year **1970**

On 22 January suggested Willy Brandt negotiations on the relations between the two German states to Willi Stoph, who was the chairman of the "Ministerrat" (cabinet council) of the GDR (DDR). The same day visited the Polish Foreign Minister Burakiewicz as first member of a communist government of Poland the Federal Republic of Germany (West Germany). This official visit followed within the scope of the German-Polish economic negotiations. Only a few days later Egon Bahr, who was permanent secretary of the "Bundeskanzleramt" (Federal Chancellery of West Germany), went to Moscow to enter into secret talks about a nonaggression treaty. All that already showed that West Germany's focal point was the east policy.

On 1 February was made a treaty about deliveries of Soviet natural gas to West Germany. West Germany should deliver the pipes for the pipeline of this gas. Only a few days later were started secrets talks about the normalization of mutual relations between West Germany and Poland in Warsaw, the capital of Poland.

On 10 February followed the first international terrorist attack in West Germany. In Munich was an aeroplane of the Israeli airline El Al attacked by terrorists. During this attack died one Israeli and 11 passengers were injured. Only three days later followed an arson attack in a Jewish old people's home in Munich, seven old persons lost their life. That was the prelude to other assassinations in West Germany.

On 19 March Willy Brandt visited officially the DDR and met Willi Stoph, the chairman of the cabinet council (Ministerrat) of the

German Democratic Republic (GDR/DDR), there in Erfurt (today capital of the country Thuringia). It was the first meeting of heads of government of two German states. The people of the GDR (DDR) gave Willy Brandt, the chancellor of West Germany, an enthusiastic reception; this was unpleasant to the political leadership of the DDR, because it showed that the people of the DDR were longing to reunification.

On 31 March was the German ambassador, Karl Maria Graf von Spreti, kidnapped by terrorists in Guatemala. On 5 April he was found then, he was dead. The terrorists had demanded the release of several political convicts, but the government of Guatemala had rejected that. This was the death sentence to Karl Maria Graf von Spreti. When the terrorists received the information of no release of their political friends, they killed him immediately.

For some months was active a new terror group in West Germany, the **RAF** (**R**ote **A**rmee **F**raktion/Red Army Faction). When the leading head of the APO, Rudi Dutschke, was seriously injured during an attempt on his life in April of the year of 1968, dropped the assault power of this movement (APO) off. It was divided into several politically strategic discussion groups with socialist, communist or anarchist tendency. A little group of radicals prepared especially for the revolution in the Federal Republic of Germany. Andreas Baader and Horst Mahler formed together with the journalist Ulrike Meinhof and the student Gudrun Ensslin the hard core of the "Rote Armee Fraktion" **(Baader-Meinhof-Group/Gang)**. The goal of this group of the **RAF** was, to "tear away the mask from the face of the fascist state (so these terrorists called West Germany) by provocative violence". By it these terrorists wanted to "bring about conditions for a real national uprising to initiate a just society".

During the first phase, 1967 – 1970, was the **RAF** a kind of catalyst. Then there was a phase of peace for a short time, because Andreas Baader had been arrested in the meantime. On 14 May of this year he could escape, but there was still peace till the second phase of action of the **RAF**. This second phase covered the years 1972 – 1975, in which developed especially successive organizations of the **RAF**, so the **"Bewegung 2. Juni"** (Movement June 2) and the **"Revolutionären Zellen"** (Revolutionary Cells). The cause of this development was the complete elimination of the hard core of the **RAF**. During the second phase the lawyers of the arrested hard core of the **RAF** had played a part in the building up of a second **RAF**-generation and the development of new information net. The third period (1976/77) was determined by actions of the second **RAF**-generation with the murders of Siegfried Buback, Jürgen Ponto and Hanns-Martin Schleyer. The suicides of Ulrike Meinhof and Gudrun Ensslin, Andreas Baader and Jan-Carl Raspe, which happened also within this period, meant the end of the first **RAF**-generation. The chief characteristic of the fourth phase (from 1978 on) was the decrease of the "left-wing terrorism" as a result of an effective fight against this group, was a certain revival of the right-wing extremism and the probable organization of a third **RAF**-generation.

The new government of West Germany under Chancellor Willy Brandt started with its east political activities in this year. But this east policy was the same policy, which had also made the previous government. Gerhard Schröder, the Foreign Minister under Chancellor Ludwig Erhard, had already searched stubbornly for new ways of understanding with the East European states, but that without sweeping success. Previously he had carefully undermined the "Hallstein-Doktrin", the claim to sole representation, for this purpose. The first step to the recognition of "a state DDR" (GDR/German Democratic Republic) was done when the "great coalition" of West Germany considered to "negotiate directly" with the head of government of the DDR/GDR. There was besides no serious group, which laid claim to the (former) "East Regions of Germany" (Silesia, East Pomerania and East Prussia) in view of Hitler's war against Poland and the cruelties of the Nazis there. But officially belonged these regions still to Germany and were a political object in dispute. Now there was a possibility of the solution to the question of borderline in the wind, the new West German government aimed at the recognition of the Oder-Neisse-line as Germany's frontier, as it was also required by the Catholic and Protestant Church of Germany. Now the new east policy had to fit also in an international course of détente, so that no government of West Germany could remove from this course in the long run.

The initiative of the new West German government was nevertheless a courageous step. This step could deserve credit only, if also the other side respected the realties, the real political situation in the middle of Europe. For example: the tie of West Berlin to the Federal Republic of Germany (West Germany). Berlin was still a political crisis centre of the world. Any presence of West Germany in West Berlin was fought by the East by means of protests and harassment at the access roads from West Germany to West Berlin. There was no rule of the civil access, which was approved by all victorious powers. But Brandt and Scheel didn't want to see the settlement with the East alone in connection of performance and return. West Germany couldn't lose by concessions in their opinion. The point was 25 years after the capitulation of "Hitler-Germany", to say goodbye to the illusions of the "era of Adenauer" and – also to the West – to find out about the goals of the German policy. The offensive of détente had really led to an unprecedented upgrading of the West German foreign politics. It seemed for two or three years that the problem "Germany" would be a focal point of the international politics.

During the negotiations about the conclusion of a "German-Soviet nonaggression treaty" in January, Egon Bahr, the (West) German negotiating leader, had to experience that the continuation of the talks was put at risk by a flood of indiscretions. It was mainly negotiated about the question of the German east frontier; the Soviets urged West Germany to accept finally the border between the German Democratic Republic (DDR) and the (former) east regions of Germany as new frontier between Germany and Poland, whilst the government of West Germany had to keep the option of a change open, because the (West) German constitution included a rule of reunion of the whole of Germany. The West German Foreign Minister, Walter Scheel, was facing his Soviet colleague in office, Andrej Gromyko, in the end. Andrej Gromyko was a hard-boiled diplomat, but Walter Scheel, who was an underestimated "rheinische Frohnatur" (cheerful person of the Rhineland) and was always in Brandt's shadow, could shake off his reputation for being a political lightweight. He negotiated with success. On 12 August signed Brandt and Scheel the treaty.

15 years after Adenauer's difficult Moscow mission, which was still darkened by the shadow of the past, had travelled a head of government from Bonn into the centre of the communist world

again. But this time there had been a lot of talk about cooperation and reconciliation, the talk turned above all to the subject "economic cooperation". Now the (West) German industry was on the side of the new east policy of the government because of own interest. The heart of the treaty of Moscow was the third "article": "Die vertragsschließenden Seiten betrachten heute und künftig die Grenzen aller Staaten in Europa als unverletzlich, wie sie am Tage der Unterzeichnung dieses Vertrages verlaufen, einschließlich der Oder-Neiße-Linie, die die Westgrenze der Volksrepublick Polen bildet, und der Grenze zwischen der Bundesrepublik Deutschland und der Deutschen Demokratischen Republik"(Today and in future both sides of this treaty consider the frontiers of all states in Europe as inviolable; so the day of signing of this treaty is decisive for the frontier also between Germany and the People's Republic Poland, i.e., the Oder-Neisse-line is inviolable today and in future too. West Germany respects also the border with the German Democratic Republic). This recognition was regarded by the Soviet Union as confirmation of its conquests during the Second World War and its executive role in East Europe. From Germany's point of view was renounced a forcible border change, but it wasn't ruled out the possibility of a peaceful revision. The (West) German Foreign Minister announced in his letter "zur deutschen Einheit" (for the German unity) to his Soviet colleague in office, Gromyko, that this treaty wasn't inconsistent with the political goals of the Federal Republic of Germany, which worked towards a state of peace in Europe, in which the German nation regains its unity by free self-determination. The West German government and the west powers exchanged furthermore letters (notes) with the establishing that according to the view of the parties to this agreement, so also according to the view of the Soviet Union, wouldn't be concerned the question of the right and responsibility of the four super powers regarding Germany as whole. By it was the "Treaty of Moscow" not inconsistent with the rule of reunification according to the opinion of the West German government; this treaty wouldn't be inconsistent with the reservation of a treaty of peace too, said the West Germans.

On 7 December signed Brandt and Scheel a "German-Polish treaty" in Warsaw. Also here was set the formula of the "inviolable frontier Oder-Neisse" (but not as final frontier between Germany and Poland!) and it was stated the renunciation of territorial claims, because Silesia, East Pomerania and East Prussia were still German provinces according to the opinion of the West German government (but from Polish point of view already West Polish territories). The negotiations with Poland didn't take a normal course too. There were hard negotiations for both sides. The problem of resettlement of thousands and thousands of Germans, who were still living in Silesia, East Pomerania and East Prussia, could be only solved after the year of 1975, when the chancellor of those days, Helmut Schmidt, promised a credit of 1,000,000,000 DM. Now the Germans, who agreed to give up their home there, could leave these (former) German territories. – There was a special scene of emotion on the occasion of the signing of the "Treaty of Warsaw". Willy Brandt kneeled down before the monument to the victims of the revolt in the ghetto of Warsaw. It was an act of human and moral-political greatness at the beginning of politics, which aimed at understanding. The picture with Brandt, which showed him kneeling down before the monument, went round the world.

We write the year **1971**

The Federal Republic of Germany entered into several diplomatic relations with East European states in this year. During the negotiations with Czechoslovakia arose the question, since when the "Agreement of Munich" of the year of 1938 (agreement about the cession of the "Sudetenland", which was forced on Czechoslovakia) should be declared null and void: from the beginning or from a later time? The government in Bonn had to take the "later time", because sovereign acts by German public authorities and German courts of justice had been otherwise contestable and a flood of actions for damages had been possible too. But the most important point of the negotiations with Czechoslovakia was that the "Agreement of Munich" was declared null and void at all.

On September 3 the four Allies made the agreement on Berlin, the so-called "Vier-Mächte-Abkommen". Walter Scheel, the West German Foreign Minister, had the coming into force of the Treaty of Moscow made dependent on a satisfactory settlement on Berlin. A satisfactory settlement on Berlin was thus the condition of the signing of the "Treaty of Moscow". By it was accepted the tie of West Berlin to West Germany for the first time by the Soviet Union.

The agreement on West Berlin led to obligatory rules for the connecting ways to this city, to travel possibilities for inhabitants of West Berlin to East Berlin and into the DDR, as well as to other practical agreements, by which the situation of West Berlin was improved.

On 20 October received Willy Brandt the Peace Nobel Prize for his east policy and politics of détente. He was the fourth German, who received this prize, after Gustav Stresemann (1926), Ludwig Quidde (1927) and Carl von Ossietzky (1935).

The CDU/CSU found it hard to must take leave of the government in West Germany after 20 years, whilst the SPD could achieve successes as ruling party. Many members of the CDU/CSU weren't prepared to accept to part as opposition, which was assigned to them. Their hope of a swift recovery of the government focussed on Rainer Barzel, the intelligent and eloquent party leader of the CDU, thought him capable of a tricky mission too. Now the point was, to turn the bare majority of the government of only 12 votes to a majority for a chancellor of the CDU by "deserters", above all from the conservative wing of the FDP. But this operation could be successful only if there was an extra-parliamentary approval for it, if the change was enough legitimized. This reason of justification presented the passionate opposition against the new east policy now. The CDU/CSU was convinced that the own party would have reached more if one of the own party had carried on the negotiations instead of Brandt and Scheel, who had negotiated hastily and sloppily. The opposition referred rightly to the settlement of the German east frontier to be a final frontier now; but that wasn't the interpretation of the West German government after negotiations with the Soviet Union and Poland. The opinion of the opposition also was that the goal of a reunification was eroded by the "Treaties of Moscow and Warsaw".

Whilst a part of the CDU/CSU didn't attack the fundamental right of the treaties, but attacked the modalities of these treaties, there were also uncompromising adversaries among the own ranks of both parties, who fought against each acceptance of the status quo as capitulation to the Soviet striving for power.

Many of these adversaries also argued morally. The communist systems of injustice were no partners with equal rights to them.

On May 3 of this year was relieved Walter Ulbricht of his duties as "First Secretary" of the central committee of the DDR by Erich Honecker. That stood for new politics. Honecker didn't have Ulbricht's dream about a "sozialistische Menschengemeinschaft" (socialist human community), he didn't want to build up by all means a socialist ideal state, a model state, within a short time. Honecker was pragmatist. He wanted that the inhabitants of the DDR can identify themselves with the social system of the DDR within the bounds of possibility. He tried to secure the supply with consumer goods, he imported from the West what he couldn't get in the East – machines, ladies' boots, automobiles or bananas – he announced a socialist programme and declared for the house building, the so-called "Plattenbau" (slab building), as the most important project aim.

We write the year **1972**

On 24 January rejected the "Bundesausschuss der CDU" (parliamentary committee of the party CDU of the Federal Republic of Germany) the "east treaties". But there were also members of the SPD, who didn't agree to these treaties. So Herbert Hupka, a Member of Parliament of the SPD, went over to the CDU in protest against the east policy of the West German government on 28 February. In the spring the SPD/FDP-government had still a majority of four in the parliament of the Federal Republic of Germany (West Germany). On 23 April Rainer Barzel, the new candidate of the CDU for the chancellorship, could be sure about two other Members of Parliament of the party FDP and a third Member of Parliament of the FDP went even over to the CDU.

Now it seemed that Barzel could be sure about the majority for the election as chancellor. The day after, the CDU/CSU moved for a motion of no confidence against the acting chancellor Willy Brandt according to "Artikel 67" of the West German constitutional law (Grundgesetz) On 27 April followed the voting by ballot then. When the result was made known Rainer **Barzel** could only shake his head. 247 Members of Parliament had voted for him, 10 had voted against him and 3 had abstained from voting, i.e., almost each of the Members of Parliament of the parties SPD and FDP had boycotted this voting. According to the result had at least 2 Members of Parliament of the CDU/CSU voted against Rainer Barzel. The vote of no confidence had thus no success for the CDU/CSU, because of missing majority (because also the absent Members were included for the result of the voting). One of the both Members of Parliament, who had voted against Barzel, disclosed his identity later. He took bribes of 50,000 DM according to what he said, but that was never cleared up. After the vote of confidence was the "Bundestag" (West German Parliament) dissolved according to "Artikel 68" of the constitutional law and a date for a new election fixed. The SPD proclaimed this new election plebiscite of its east policy.

On 26 May was the first treaty of international law signed between both German states. By this treaty, the so-called "Verkehrsvertrag", the technical details of the trade between both states were regulated and was made the departure of inhabitants of the DDR easier in case of urgent family affairs. Everybody could identify with humanitarian relief. The east policy got into an uplift of mood again, which also did not slacken when the Federal Republic of Germany awarded to the German Democratic Republic (DDR) the sovereignty, which was denied for a long time, by a "Grundlagenvertrag". By this treaty was intended to develop normal neighbourly relations on the basis of equal rights and inviolable borders. The government in Bonn (West Germany) pronounced thus, that the present "Zonengrenze" (zone's border) was an official frontier between two sovereign states now. West Germany renounced also the "Alleinvertretungsanspruch" (claim to sole representation) and agreed upon the simultaneous admission of both German states in the United Nations, which then followed in the next year. The DDR got rid with it of the last hurdles of an international presence. But the "Grundlagenvertrag" contained also wordings, which approached to the "construction of exceptional relations" of the West German government. In the preamble to this "Basic Treaty" was given expressly a mention of dissension in some points, for example also the question about "one nation". Both German states exchanged "ständige Vertretungen" (constant representatives) and no ambassadors. The treaty said above all nothing about the question of citizenship. Thus was furthermore guaranteed the principle that every German, also a citizen of the DDR, could claim the diplomatic protection and the rights of the Federal Republic of Germany. – Legal reservations were confirmed by an exchange of notes like the exchange of notes on the treaties of Moscow and Warsaw.

When on 8 November the "Grundlagenvertrag" was published, the "Bundestag" was already dissolved and the electoral battle in the final phase. But now the surprising and very promising agreement with the DDR got of course "following wind" for the governing parties. The election of 19 November won the SPD, became strongest party now and could thus displaced the "Union" (= CDU/CSU); also the FDP could gain a solid basis.

On 6 February of this year had begun the big acts of terrorism in West Germany. In Brühl close to Cologne were 5 Jordanians murdered. The culprits, so was guessed, were members of a Palestinian organization of terrorism. West Germany was already covered by series of fire and bomb attacks in the year of 1970. These attacks were directed against judges, politicians and high American military personnel in West Germany, thus against representatives of the "Western System". But also many other persons were attacked by accident, without predetermined purpose. In summer the arrests of the leading heads of the RAF (Red Army Faction), amongst them were Baader, Ensslin, Meinhof, Meins and Raspe, didn't bring unexpectedly reliefs. The "hard core" managed the work of a General Staff out of the prisons, some lawyers organized committees of support and defence to recruit sympathizers and activists.

For a long time German terrorists took action abroad and international terrorist groups took action in West Germany, often they had contact with each other. On 5 September, an unbelievable occurrence happened in Munich. The Olympic Games, which should be "cheerful games", were abruptly held up. Palestinian terrorists had committed an attempt on the life of the members of the Israelite Olympic team. The terrorists could escape from the Olympic Village with the entire Israelite Olympic team by force of arms. In Fürstenfeldbruck, a little town close to Munich, they were taken on then. The attempt to rescue by the Bavarian police ended in a massacre, 17 persons were killed, amongst them the most members of the Israelite Olympic team and some terrorists. The Olympic Games were continued after funeral obsequies in spite of reservations, but now there were no cheerful games, now there were games of dismay. – Because the Bavarian police had taken no skilful action against the terrorists, the West German government took now occasion to found special anti-terrorism forces. Thus was founded the special unit "**GSG** 9" (**G**renz**S**chutz **G**ruppe 9/frontier protection group 9), which took worldwide actions in the following years, contrary to its name "Frontier Protection Group". In this group/unit are only young soldiers, who were trained to be fighters of a task force against terrorists.

When 1969 the statesman General de Gaulle, who had blocked the European integration, quitted the political scene, but had also to serve as "Sündenbock" (sin buck) for national egoism of other nations, the Europeans were urged to act. So on 1 and 2 December 1969 the summit conference of the 6 heads of state and government of the European Community (EG) in The Hague (Den Haag/Netherlands) had decided to realize an "economic and currency union" till 1980. The new currency should be the "Euro" then. But the worldwide economic crisis of the year of 1971, which had different aftereffects to the 6 member states of the European Community (France, Italy, the Netherlands, Belgium, Luxembourg and West Germany), questioned this intention and these six states didn't really introduce a common currency too.

On 21 December signed the West German minister Egon Bahr and the permanent secretary of the DDR, Michael Kohl, who belonged to the "Ministerrat" (cabinet council), the "Grundlagenvertrag" (Basic Treaty) about the relations between both German states. That happened in East Berlin.

We write the year **1973**

On 1 January increased the number of member states of the European Community. Denmark, Ireland and Great Britain became members of the Community; now the European Community had a total of 9 members.

On 18 January made the West German chancellor, Willy Brandt, his policy statement in parliament. He announced the continuation of the foreign policy on the basis of neighbourly relations. His goals were also more social justice and interior reforms.

On 11 May the "Bundestag" agreed with the majority of the government to the "Basic Treaty" about the interior-German relations. The "Bundesverfassungsgericht" (Federal Constitutional Court) – the Bavarian government had appealed to this highest court of West Germany – declared the treaty about the interior-German relations to be compatible with the "Grundgesetz" (constitutional law of West Germany). But this court fixed also a whole of string of items, thus the opinion that the "German Empire" had survived relating to international law and would be identical with the Federal Republic of Germany (West Germany) now. The frontier between both German states would be also a border like the borders between the West German countries. Few months later the DDR took occasion of this award of the West German constitutional court to cancel all mentions of an united nation in the own (new) constitution.

In the time between 18 and 22 May visited the secretary general of the Communist Party of the Soviet Union, Leonid Brezhnev, the West German capital Bonn; there he met Willy Brandt for talks about the Soviet-German relations.

On 1 August died Walter Ulbricht in East Berlin. He, the leader of the party SED and chairman of the "Staatsrat" (state/cabinet council) of the DDR, died at the age of 80. He had lost his post as First Secretary of the SED in the year of 1971 because of his resistance to the rapprochement between West Germany and the socialist states of East Europe by the east policy of Willy Brandt. Walter Ulbricht was always an East German opponent of this West German policy contrary to his own party in East Germany (DDR), which was seeking for a rapprochement. Therefore he was politically deprived of his power too.

On 7 December was agreed upon during the political talks between the Polish Foreign Minister Olszowski and the West German government in Bonn that 50,000 Germans could leave Silesia, East Pomerania and the western part of East Prussia, but in those days there were still living some hundred thousand Germans.

We write the year **1974**

On 23 January decided the West Germany government to set up a Department of the Environment in West Berlin. The government of the German Democratic Republic (DDR) protested against the setting up of this department. But the government of West Germany didn't pay attention to this protest and realized its project.

On 8 March suffered the east policy of West Germany a heavy defeat. The "Bundesrat" (Upper House of the West German Parliament) rejected the German-Czech "Treaty of Normalisation" by the votes of the countries, which were ruled by the CDU/CSU. The number of expellees from Bohemia and Moravia (Czech

Rep.) was especially large in Bavaria; there ruled the CSU. These expellees, the "Sudeten", voted for the most part for the CSU.

On 22 April was Richard von Weizsäcker appointed candidate of the CDU to the post of the "Bundespräsident" (President of West Germany) – There was an incredible occurrence only two days later in West Germany. Günter Guillaume, the personal assistant to the West German chancellor, Willy Brandt, was arrested together with his wife. They were suspected of having spied for the DDR/GDR. Günter Guillaume admitted having done it and to be "Hauptmann der Nationalen Volksarmee der DDR" (captain of the National People's Army of the German Democratic Republic/GDR). That was the cause for Willy Brandt's resignation from this post as chancellor of West Germany on May 6. New chancellor of the Federal Republic of Germany became Helmut Schmidt (SPD) now. New vice-chancellor and Foreign Minister of West Germany became Hans-Dietrich Genscher.

On 15 May was Walter Scheel (FDP) elected President of the Federal Republic of Germany (West Germany). That happened by the "Bundesversammlung" (Federal Assembly of all Members of the West German Parliament and people's representatives from the West German countries to elect the West German President). Walter Scheel was counter-candidate of Richard von Weizsäcker, who lost this election.

On 7 October came the new constitution of the DDR into force. All indications of a reunification of both of the German states were finally cancelled in this constitution. Many states, amongst them also the U.S.A., recognized the DDR as independent state now.

On 13 September some members of the terror group "Baader-Meinhof", who were under arrest, had gone on hunger strike. On 9 November died Holger Meins, one of the arrested members of this terror group, as a result of the hunger strike in spite of force feeding. The members of the RAF said now that Holger Meins was murdered. That was also the cause that they killed the "Kammergerichtspräsident" (President of the Chamber Court) of West Berlin, von Drenkmann, one day later. Von Drenkmann had been kidnapped by the RAF short time before.

Helmut Schmidt, German Chancellor 1974-1982

We write the year **1975**

On 5 February the members of the Baader-Meinhof group, of those who were arrested, called off their hunger strike. They had seen that they couldn't reach their goal by such strike. On 27 February was Peter Lorenz, the chairman of the CDU of West Berlin, kidnapped by members of the terror group "Bewegung 2. Juni". They demanded the release of their members, of those who were under arrest, and succeeded. Then two months later there was an attack on the (West) German embassy in Stockholm/Sweden. The attackers had taken the successful blackmail in case of Peter Lorenz as an example. But the West German government stood this time firm. An explosion of bombs, which was released by mistake, brought the attack to an end then. On 21 May were the leaders of the terror group "Baader-Meinhof", Andreas Baader, Ulrike Meinhof, Gudrun Ensslin and Jan-Carl Raspe, put on trial in Stuttgart-Stammheim.

On 19 June became Helmut Kohl, who was Minister-President of the country Rhineland-Palatinate, candidate of the CDU/CSU for the chancellorship to the next election, which should be held in 1976. Then, June 23, he became also party leader of the CDU. That happened during the party conference of the CDU in Mannheim (an industrial town on the river Rhine).

On 3 August signed the party leader of the Communist Party of Poland, Gierek, and the new chancellor of West Germany, Helmut Schmidt, an agreement that settled the Polish claims on the pension scheme of West Germany and questions about leaving Poland, because many Germans, who were still living in the (former) East German regions, intended to got to West Germany.

On 20 August committed the terror organization RAF (Rote Armee Fraktion/Red Army Faction) a bomb attack on the chairman of the Jewish community of West Berlin, Heinz Galinski. Galinski might thank his lucky stars that he wasn't killed by the bomb, he remained uninjured.

On 9 September were the terrorists arrested, who were involved in the kidnapping of Lorenz. These terrorists were: Ralf Reinders, Inge Viett and Juliane Plambeck. On 13 September was also Fritz Teufel, who belonged to the same terror group, arrested.

On 15 December was Günter Guillaume, who was spy of the DDR and who has caused the resignation of Willy Brandt as chancellor, sentenced to 13 year's imprisonment, his wife Christel to 8 year's imprisonment. They were taken to court in Düsseldorf, there, where they were sentenced now.

We write the year **1976**

On 3 January was the German coast of the North Sea heavily storm-flood-ridden again. A large part of the coast area of Schleswig-Holstein was flooded, 16 persons drowned in the waters. Only a few days later another catastrophe occurred in North Germany. In Hamburg exploded a cauldron in the area of the harbour, 26 persons lost their life.

On 9 May Ulrike Meinhof hung up herself in her cell of the prison of Stuttgart-Stammheim. Her suicide could be considered as physic exhaustion, particularly since the pressure amongst the members of the terror group got more and more gruelling; her suicide was perhaps also a mark of political resignation. But her fanatic followers said: "It was murder". Only a few days later the

West German government passed the "Verfahrensregeln zur Abwehr von Extremisten im öffentlichen Dienst" (procedural rules for the warding off of extremists in the civil service). By these procedural rules was the "Radikalenerlass" (Decree against Radicals) of the year of 1972 removed.

On 1 June was committed a bomb attack against the HQ of the American Army in Frankfurt. But there were fortunately no dead persons. It was an attack of the RAF supposed. The RAF hadn't appeared in this year, but that was to change in the following year.

On 7 July died the former President of West Germany, Gustav Heinemann. He was 76 years old. The same day escaped the terrorists Inge Viett, Gabriele Rollnik, Juliane Plambeck and Monika Berberich from the women's prison of West Berlin. It is safe to assume that they had helpers for escaping. That was also the reason now that Hermann Oxfort, a member of the party FDP, resigned his post as Senator of Justice of West Berlin four days later.

We write the year **1977**

On 19 March was demonstrated against the construction of nuclear power stations in West Germany, as it happened often in the last time. This time demonstrated many people against the construction of the nuclear power station of Grohnde on the river Weser. Now there were heavy riots during this demonstration and some hundred persons were injured.

On 7 April was Siegfried Buback, who was "Generalbundesanwalt" (Chief State Prosecutor of West Germany), murdered by terrorists. With him were killed his driver Wolfgang Göbel and one security officer. The culprits belonged to the terror group "Kommando Ulrike-Meinhof-Rote-Armee-Fraktion", a splinter group of the RAF. Siegfried Buback was 57 years old. On 30 July followed the next terrorist attack of the RAF. Jürgen Ponto, who was chairman of the Board of the "Deutsche Bank", opened the front door of this villa. He was ahead of Susanne Albrecht, a good-acquainted woman, in this moment; therefore he didn't fear the worst. But Susanne Albrecht was accompanied by other persons, terrorists of the RAF. Jürgen Ponto should be kidnapped, but he defended himself and was shot dead. Then on 5 September the next attack of the RAF. Hanns-Martin Schleyer, who was President of the Employers' Association of West Germany, was kidnapped. His driver and three security officers were killed at this attack. This time the West German government was going on time gained in contrast to the kidnapping of Lorenz. Now government and opposition worked together in one crisis management group. Six weeks later, on October 13, hijacked Palestinian terrorists the "Landshut", a passenger aeroplane of the Lufthansa. This hijack occurred on the Spanish island Majorca. The "Landshut" was hijacked to Mogadishu (capital of Somalia/East Africa). The terrorists wanted to force the release of all leading heads of their terror group by it; also they wanted to lay stress on the blackmail attempts of the kidnapping of Schleyer. In Mogadishu came the GSG 9, which was founded as anti-terror group after the assassination during the Olympic Games of Munich as we know, to the hostages' rescue. The men of the GSG 9 took by storm the "Landshut" and killed the most Palestinian terrorists. That happened only five days after the hijack of this aeroplane. Now there was every reason to believe that the success of the anti-terror group GSG 9 caused also the suicides of Gudrun Ensslin, Andreas Baader and Jan-Carl Raspe in the prison of Stuttgart-Stammheim. Baader and Raspe shot themselves by revolvers, which they had smuggled into the prison before. Now their suicides looked like murders. New acts of revenge should be provoked by it. The suicides in Stuttgart-Stammheim caused now that Hanns-Martin Schleyer was killed by the terrorists. His dead body was found on 19 October in Mühlhausen/Mulhouse (Alsace/France). The body was in a boot of a parking car. The responsible politicians had put up with these consequences. Their decision had been credible, if there wouldn't be the mishaps of tracing and search actions and wouldn't be the scandal that arrested terrorists had revolvers at their disposal.

After the murder of Hanns-Martin Schleyer the actions of the terrorists decreased noticeable. The terrorists had to see that the West German state wasn't open to blackmails, but was ready to esteem highly the security of the society and the state authority in an emergency. In this case was that more worth to the state than a human life. It was a very bitter, but also necessary act of the state discipline.

We write the year **1978**

On 16 February the West German parliament had passed new anti-terror laws, which gave more possibilities of the police to the search for terrorists.

In this year united also the states of the "**E**uropean **C**ommunity" (**EC**/EG), with exception of Great Britain, into the "**E**uropean **M**onetary **S**ystem" (**EMS/EWS** = Europäisches Währungs-System). Within this monetary bloc were fixed rates of exchange, but which could be removed by revaluation or devaluation. During the summit conference of The Hague (Den

Haag/Netherlands) was decided that all states of the European Community should join the monetary bloc, also Norway that didn't belong to the European Community. So all states of the community also did it, with exception of Great Britain; also Norway rejected to join. The fierce arguments within each state of the community, under which the partners of the monetary bloc executed the joining of this bloc, gave a foretaste of future ordeals. On 21 April the "Bundestag" passed the law on the direct voting on the Members of the European Parliament. The first European poll should be held between 7 and 10 June 1979. Up to now were the Members of the European Parliament appointed by each member state.

On 24 September were two other terrorists of the RAF arrested in Dortmund, their names: Angelika Speitel and Michael Knoll.

We write the year **1979**

On 20 January were 5 scientists arrested in West Germany; they had spied for the DDR. That caused new political tensions between the German Democratic Republic (DDR) and the Federal Republic of Germany (West Germany). The consequences were now that the western journalists were very much hindered in doing their job in the DDR; interviews had to be approved from now. Contacts with western reporters were stricter supervised. Also the circulation of western currency was restricted for monetary transactions.

On 22 January started the West German TV station with the U.S.-American series "Holocaust". These series described the fate of a Jewish family in Germany during the time of the Nazis and showed the extermination of the Jews by the Nazi-rulers.

Many Germans followed with great attention these series; they couldn't believe that such cruelties really happened in Germany. The Nazis had understood to cover their cruelties from the German population. The defeat of Nazi-Germany brought the cruelties of the Nazis to light only. Whilst the series "Holocaust" were televised, committed some right-wing extremists bomb attacks on television stations in West Germany.

On 16 February was a former lawyer of Baader and Meinhof sentenced in Stuttgart. It was Klaus Croissant, who was brought to trial because of the support of a criminal association, therefore he was sentenced to an imprisonment of 2 ½ years. He got addition to it a ban on pursuing his career for 4 years.

On 4 May was shot a suspect terrorist during a police search in Nuremberg (Nürnberg). It was Elisabeth von Dyck, who was suspect to be involved with the murder of Hanns-Martin Schleyer.

On 23 May elected the "Bundesversammlung" the new President of West Germany. The new President became Karl Carstens now; he was the fifth President of the Federal Republic of Germany. Before he was "Bundestagspräsident" (Speaker of the Bundestag) Karl Carstens's successor as "Speaker of the Bundestag" became Richard Stücklen, a member of the party CSU (the Bavarian Christian Party). Then on 1 July was Karl Carstens sworn in the post as President of the Federal Republic of Germany. Only a few days later elected the CDU/CSU Franz-Josel Strauß candidate for the chancellorship of these two parties. The next election to the "Bundestag" should be held in 1980.

In July was abolished by the "Bundestag" the law on the period of limitation for murder; by it the state had the possibility now, to continue prosecuting war crimes. Many Nazi-criminals were not yet sentenced, because the state couldn't get hold of them up to now. But the West German authority hoped that it will be done as quickly as possible in the near future.

On 12 December decided the board of the NATO, to deploy new nuclear medium-range missiles, Pershing II and Cruise Missiles, from the end of the year of 1983 in Europe and that above all in West Germany. The reason should be, to fill the gap of deterrence, which came into being by the Soviet previous armament. So should also be saved the "strategy of the flexible answer". This decision was coupled to the offer to the Soviet Union, to negotiate on a new arms control, of which purpose should be the full renunciation (zero option) of medium-range missiles (double resolution).

Two famous writers

Heinrich Böll

Heinrich Böll was born on 21 December 1917 in Cologne; he died on 16 July 1985 in Langenbroich-Kreuzau (Eifel). Heinrich Böll was at first a bookseller, 1939 – 1945 soldier and since 1947 writer. In his successful works he described often sharply, now and then satirically, the reality of the everyday life during the war, the reality of the post-war years, of the "Wirtschaftswunder" (period of economic miracle) and the reality of the institutions of state and church. His Catholic faith didn't prevent him from writing about radical-critical subjects. – **Stories:** "Der Zug war pünktlich" 1949; "Wanderer, kommst du nach Spa......." 1950; "Wo warst du, Adam?" 1951; "Das Brot der frühen Jahre" 1955; "Entfernung von der Truppe" 1954; "Ende einer Dienstfahrt" 1966; "Die verlorene Ehre der Katharina Blum" 1976; "Die Verwundung" 1983. **Novels:** " Und sagte kein einziges Wort" 1953; "Haus ohne Hüter"; "Billard um halb zehn" 1959; "Ansichten eines Clowns" 1963; "Gruppenbild mit Dame" 1971; "Fürsorgliche Belagerung" 1979; "Frauen vor Flußlandschaft" 1985. **Satire:** "Doktor Murkes gesammeltes Schweigen" 1958. **Drama:** "Ein Schluck Erde" 1961. Heinrich Böll wrote also many **radio and television plays**, so "Irisches Tagebuch" 1957; "Frankfurter Vorlesungen (zur Ästhetik des Humanen)" 1966; "essays, criticisms, speeches" 1967; "Reports on the mind of the nation" 1975; "Einmischung erwünscht. Schriften zur Zeit" 1977 (Interference desired. Writings for the time); an autobiographical sketch by Böll was "Was soll aus dem Jungen bloß werden?" 1981 (What only will become of the boy?). Heinrich Böll got the Nobel Literature Prize in 1972. 1971 – 1974 he was president/chairman of the international PEN Club. Böll belonged to the great men of the world literature of the years after the "Second World War" like Günter Grass.

Heinrich Böll; he worked on the history of the early Federal Republic of Germany and the silence about the Nazi period like no other author. Unmistakably connected were literary creation and political engagement of this passionate man. This, creation and political engagement, he always applied primarily to the disadvantaged and deported in society.

Günter Grass

Günter Grass was born on 16 October 1927 in the former German city Danzig (today Gdansk, a Polish city). He was training as a stonemason and studied sculpture. He lived 1946 – 1952 in Düsseldorf and 1956 – 1960 in Paris, then in West Berlin, later then in the country Schleswig-Holstein. The reader of his baroque-overflowed, vital, often also scurrilous, caricaturing, shocking-topical novels and stories, does not get rare the feeling of the general human narrow-mindedness; also the everyday life during the period of the National Socialism and the after-effects of this period in West Germany were sharply investigated. **Novels:** "Die Blechtrommel" 1959; "Hundejahre" 1963; "Örtlich betäubt" 1969; "Aus dem Tagebuch einer Schnecke" 1972; "Der Butt" 1977; "Die Rättin" 1986. Günter Grass wrote also many novellas and came off a graphic designer. He got the Nobel Literature Prize like Heinrich Böll.

In the year of 1960 Günter Grass had sought the direct political engagement and moved through West Germany as election speaker of the SPD. His great novel "Die Blechtrommel" was already a political book, which pressed the people hard, namely with phenomenal aggressiveness. The drumming "dreikäsehoch" (three-cheeses-tall) Oskar Matzerath decided, just three years old, to stop his growth in protest against the world of the adults. So he can watch them from the point of view of a frog. This "modern Simplicius" (Simplicius = a figure of fun of the Thirty - Year War - 1618 – 1648 - who was described as a man of changing destinies, as fool, as landsknecht, as quack, as robber, as hermit) tears the moral mask from the face of the petty bourgeois of Germany. He does it without mercy; he is also described as a character that breaks each taboo. This novel, which described such a character in a brilliant manner, produced admiration but caused also protests during its publication. Also in the novella "Katz und Maus" (1961) and the novel "Hundejahre", they form together with the famous novel "Die Blechtrommel" the trilogy of Danzig, are described critically the period of the

Third Reich (Nazi time) and the period of the German "Wirtschaftswunder" (economic miracle).

Günter Grass, writer and laureate

In Düsseldorf Günter Grass did an apprenticeship as stonemason and studied at the "Kunstakademie" (Academy of Art) sculpture. As musician he earned his money in the "old town" (downtown) of Düsseldorf

There were still other writers simultaneously with the Nobel prize winners Böll and Grass in Germany, like the authors of the DDR, Uwe Johnson (1934 – 1984), Ulrich Plenzdorf and Christa Wolf, or the West German authors Erika Runge, Günter Wallraff, Heinar Kipphardt, Rolf Hochhuth, Peter Weiss, Karin Struck and so on. Germany is remaining a country of "poets and thinkers".

The last years of "two German states"

We write the year **1980**

The new nationalistic party of Germany, the NPD, which was very successful in the end of the sixties, had sunk very low and played only the part of an unimportant splinter party in the meantime. But now grew up a new threat, little and aggressive neo-Nazi groups. These groups orientated themselves by the leader's principle (Führerprinzip). The members lived in groups. The romanticism of the camps during their conspiratorial meetings in uniform and bearing arms for the so-called "Wehrsport" (military service sport) attracted above all young people, who were fascinated by order and obedience or by friend and enemy, because they understood that as a protest against the world around. It was left a worrying question, to what extent the circle of persons, who sympathized with neo-Nazi ideas without to confess open to them, was to draw in view of an aggressive defamation of foreigners and the dissemination of the playing down of the atrocities of the "Dritte Reich" (Third Reich/Empire). The general public, which was shaken up by the broadcasting of the American TV-series "Holocaust", was brought down to earth again by self-finding out that the organized terror in Germany had still a breeding ground in spite of the horrors of the Third Reich. In August right-wing extremists got into a hostel of foreigners in Hamburg and murdered Vietnamese refugees. At the "Oktoberfest" of Munich detonated untimely a high-explosive bomb and killed 12 visitors of this greatest festival of Germany, more than 200 persons were injured. The assassin was arrested; it was Gundolf Köhler, a member of the neo-Nazi group **"Wehrsportgruppe Hoffmann".**

We write the year **1981**

In this year the **"Community of the Nine"** extended to the south, Greece joined with the **"European Community"**, also Portugal and Spain showed their readiness to join.

When there was the question of political integration, then there was also another important question, namely the question of own sovereignty. The resolution of Paris (1976), to tolerate the majority decision of the "European Council" (the conference of the heads of state and government) and to elect the Members of the European Parliament directly, was half-heartedly seen from this angle. It was seen half-heartedly therefore, because the new elected parliament took an unchanged mortgage over, which was delegated by the parliaments of the countries: the competence and control rights of the European Parliament are very restricted to the Commission and the Council of Ministers and not comparable with a representation of the people in a parliamentary democracy.

Even if the verve of the fifties was to make room for a technocratic crisis management, so there had been progress still made. That applies especially to the "Einigung von unten" (agreement from bottom), what takes place in countless partnerships between towns, universities or skittles clubs, but what wasn't to lead to see international understanding only EC-centrically (EC – European Community). Today is xenophobia still virulent in Germany, above all to Negros, Arabs and Turks.

In this year followed the protest against the NATO, as it happened often in the last years. In autumn marched 300,000 people, amongst them many young persons, towards Bonn, the capital of West Germany. It was a demonstration march from different starting points (Sternmarsch). There in Bonn they demonstrated against the decision of the NATO to close the armament gap.

In December was declared the war right in Poland. That was the end of the reformatory movement there; leading labour unionists of the labour union "Solidarity" were arrested. The crisis in Poland and the east-west tensions, which were mounting, strengthened the **SED** (**S**ozialistische **E**inheitspartei **D**eutschlands/Socialist Unit's Party of Germany – DDR/GDR -) in its course of demarcation. It manifested itself in reprisals against opposing artists and intellectuals, in arrests and denaturalizing. The head of the SED, Erich Honecker, made the progress of the détente conditional on maximum demands, the recognition of a citizenship of the DDR and full diplomatic relations by exchange of ambassadors between the two German states. In this year the DDR got "on Cold Way" by raising of the minimum amount for visitors from West Germany, to buy anything to the value of 25 DM each day during their stay in the DDR instead of 13 DM as before, that the number of visitors from West Germany went down from 3,200,000 persons (1978) to 2,100,000 persons now. The reason of the German Democratic Republic to do that was the fear of western influences on the own inhabitants. Now the East German government had also reached that the DDR had even higher revenue and that with a smaller number of visitors from West Germany.

In this time the people of West Germany got another wind. The "fear of the Germans" became an empirical verifiable fact according to a series of the magazine "Spiegel". The peace discussion played a part here just as the "Anti-Nuclear Power Movement". Also the problem of the chronic unemployment, what many people pestered, belonged to the existential questions. That wasn't alone the result of a worldwide slump in prices, the failing of investments of the German companies or their competitive disadvantages to the "low-wages countries" or industrial nations with lower social ranks like Japan. The unemployment was – although not alone – in the same way a result of the rationalization. Some hundred thousand jobs got lost for ever in the production and administration by new types of automatic machines and computers, the electronic "job killers" such as the industrial robots or the writing machines. At the same time it was missing the technical renovation, which could lead to a boom of demand on the mass markets, such as the market for automobiles and TV before, or they met with a glutted market, glutted by imports such as video recorders. The youth had above all concern with the unemployment, because the number of companies went down in the course of the concentration of business and caused thus a decline of training posts, whilst at the same time young persons of high-birth rate years pushed into apprenticeship and active life.

The "welfare state" of West Germany got itself talked about by the national indebtedness and unemployment too. The national income increased in the years between 1970 and 1981 (now) from 533,000,000,000 DM to 1,188,000,000,000 DM, but during the same time increased also the social welfare expenses from 174,000,000,000 DM to 484,000,000,000 DM. This trend was to continue in the following years.

This year (1981) was also called "the year of juvenile riots". 1980 already, during the coronation of Queen Beatrix of the Netherlands, broke violent conflicts between police and young "kroakers" (squatters) out. Their slogan: "Without accommodation no coronation". The focal points of the juvenile riots of this year were: Toxteh (Liverpool/England), Brixton (London/England), Zürich (Switzerland), Amsterdam (Netherlands) and West Berlin. But the causes were a distinguishing feature. The juvenile riots of Toxteh (England) were connected with the depressing unemployment of young persons, especially with the unemployment of young coloured people.

In Berlin and Amsterdam there could be connected the juvenile riots with the squatter's scene (kroaker's scene). But what did say that? Squatters weren't automatically violent; they called themselves without irony: "Instandbesetzer" (repairing squatters). They indicated also trouble spots in the urban development by their sheer existence, also they pointed to the contradiction between the lack of accommodation and extension of office buildings in the cities. The wilfully pursued dilapidation of building substance in some cases and the speculation with landed and house property gave rise to their criticism too.

In Zürich and some other cities of Switzerland were the violent conflicts between police and the "Bewegung" (the "Movement") the culmination of a criticism of culture and civilization, which saw the big cities "enclosed by pack ice". One of the central questions of this movement (die Bewegung/the "Movement") was: "Warum soll der Mensch zu fremden Planeten fliegen, wenn er nicht einmal die kleine Distanz von Mensch zu Mensch überwinden kann?" (Why should the man fly to unknown planets when he doesn't even can surmount the small distance between two persons?) The movement "Bewegung" (Movement) saw only in the foundation of autonomous youth centres a possibility to make the pack ice melting.

Even if there were important learning processes between the squatters and the political responsible persons in Berlin and Amsterdam – there were really serious attempts to surmount the inhospitality of the cities? The "**AJZ** (**A**llgemeines **J**ugendZentrum) in Zürich wurde geschleift, die Bewegung ist tot" (the General Youth Centre of Zurich was closed, the "Movement" is dead), so it was to hear there – were there also answered the questions of the youth, was there a reason for another feeling of life? It was, however, true that the "Bewegung" didn't know to help itself to the drug problem and so came into being intolerable conditions in the AJZ of Zürich; it was also true that the squatter's scene couldn't get separated clearly from the "guerilla diffusa", so the violent anarchists were called now.

Thus showed the juvenile riots of this year themselves as a mixture of social misery (England), criticism of culture and civilization (Switzerland) and social action (Amsterdam, Berlin), which could get hardly separated. But the juvenile riots showed also a spontaneous readiness for violence and showed the drug problems.

For the last days of this year took still place a meeting of the heads of government of the two German states. Schmidt and Honecker met in the airport of Berlin-Schönefeld (East Berlin/DDR). There German-internal problems were the matter of discussion.

We write the year **1982**

Ronald Reagan, the U.S.-American president, visited Bonn, the capital of West Germany, at Easter of this year. Now there was a moving peace rally during this visit. The Germans didn't want new modern missiles on their ground; they wished enduring peace for ever.

In this year a political change was to happen in West Germany. Unemployment, national indebtedness and the increase of a new party, the ecological party "Die Grünen" (the Greens), which decimated the social-liberal coalition, formed the scenario for the breaking of the SPD/FDP-coalition in the late summer, in the middle of the legislative period. Hans-Dietrich Genscher, the head of the FDP, aimed at this breaking for a long time and Chancellor Helmut Schmidt had brought about this breaking now, so that the real cause of this breaking is a moot point between both parties. Beneficiary of this argument within the coalition was Helmut Kohl, the candidate for the chancellorship of the CDU/CSU. He brought down Helmut Schmidt (SPD) now, 13 years after the election night with the establishment of a SPD/FDP-coalition. It was the first of the month October, a Friday, when the majority of the Members of Parliament voted for Helmut Kohl as new chancellor. All parliamentary members of the CDU/CSU and the most members of the FDP voted for him.

Within the year began the triumphant advance of a German product, the CD. This advance was started with the Swedish pop group "ABBA" in the summer time: their album "The Visitors" was put on the market as worldwide first CD, made from the synthetic material Makrolon of the company Bayer. By it began the era of the **C**ompact **D**isc (**CD**). In the following years replaced this silver-shining disc the records and the recording tapes. It was the beginning of the digitizing.

Nobody could know how this little disc would change the world in a short time. In the meantime was the disc developed further – from a music carrier into a data medium and video carrier in the form of the DVD of today. The basis material, a type of poly-carbonate, which was specially cut up, was several times modi-fied. The combine Bayer (one of the largest combines of Germa-ny), which has 30 % share of the world market, calls this material Makrolon today.

Uerdingen, a district of the city Krefeld in North Rhine-Westphalia, is the cradle of the mass production of the CD. Up to now is the factory of Bayer in Krefeld-Uerdingen, where the syn-thetic material was also developed in the year of 1953, with a production of 300,000 tons each year the "Hochburg" (strong-hold) of Makrolon, so also the stronghold for the mass produc-tion of the Compact Disc. At present is more than 900,000 tons polycarbonate used up for the production of optical data medi-ums. That is enough to produce many billion of the silver discs, because there is a need of only 16 grams of synthetic material for each CD. One CD, which is made of Makrolon (99% share), costs only a few cents. One silver disc is pressed in less than 3 seconds today. 1982 it takes 27 seconds for each CD.

Now the Compact Disc is drawing on a close and the **DVD** (**D**igi-tal **V**ersatile **D**isc) is already a favourite in many cases. The DVD has more capacity than the CD (tenfold); therefore this disc is especially used for music videos, too. HD-DVDs and blu-ray discs raise the factor of store to 100 and more. Holographic stores are the next revolution; by these stores can get pressed all data banks in form of holograms into the disc. So the reading and recording processes are getting faster by the multiple. The CD should have done its duty then. But in the next years we'll still have it.

The Swedish pop group ABBA, 1982 in Brighton, UK

The famous song of this group: "Waterloo"

We write the year **1983**

In this year were arrested right-wing extremists, who had committed bomb attacks on members of the U.S.-American army in West Germany.

Also in this year were held conferences on disarmament of the two super powers U.S.A. and Soviet Union in Geneva. During the talks with less and less hope of success started a great rebellion of the peace movement and many dedicated citizens of West Germany and other European countries against the putting up of new American and Soviet missiles: more than one million people took part in demonstrations on 22 October in West Germany; a human chain of more than 100,000 persons extended from Ulm to Stuttgart more than 100 km through Swabia, more than 300,000 persons marched to Bonn for a rally, 400,000 marched to Hamburg, 200,000 marched to Stuttgart ... The peace movement - in Germany as in other countries, above all in the U.S.A. - opposed the idea, peace could be based on deterrence. The arms race, which was necessarily related with the deterrence and that made an arsenal of nuclear weapons above all from West Germany, increased still the danger of war according to the opinion of the peace movement. No "balance of horror" but alone the disarmament would secure the peace. Some members of the peace movement also agreed a unilateral disarmament. The peace movement of the DDR (GDR), which was supported above all by young Christians, was especially noteworthy. The motto of this peace movement was: "Schwerter zu Pflugscharen" (lot of ploughs instead of swords). That met with respect all over the world. But the politics of the super powers followed own rules: the negotiations in Geneva brought no result, in November were the first Pershing II-missiles also deployed in West Germany, whilst the Soviet Union deployed own missiles in the DDR and Czechoslovakia. The armament spiral revolved thus further.

During the second half of the seventies a large ecological movement came in being in West Germany. This movement included youth organizations and the "Bürgerinitiative Umweltschutz" (Citizens' Action Group "Care of the Environment"). This new movement called itself (as already known) "Die Grünen" (The Greens); now this movement became a party. On 7 October 1979 "The Greens" had for the first time taken their seats in a parliament of a West German country: with 5.14% of the votes they had seats in Parliament of Bremen (= Senate of Bremen, because Bremen is a city state like Hamburg and Berlin). The Greens had other successes after that and had also seats in the parliaments of Baden-Württemberg, Berlin (senate), Lower Saxony and Hessen. Since this year, March 6, they were sitting also in "Bundestag" (parliament of West Germany). The political culture had changed by this development in West Germany, because the Germans had to prepare themselves for a new type of political representations of interests in the meantime: "the social movements". There was understood under "social movements": the "Anti-Nuclear-Movement", the "Ecology-Movement", the "Peace-Movement", the "Third-World-Initiatives", "Citizen-Initiatives", the "Alternative Movement" including squatter's scene, but also fighting minorities like homosexuals, religious minorities, handicapped persons and many other groups belonged to the "social movements". But the most successful movement of those days was the "Frauenbewegung" (women's liberation), a movement with tradition.

Helmut Kohl, German Chancellor 1982-1998

We write the year **1984**

The affair Kießling and a party donation scandal shocked the people of West Germany.

On 1 January was the "four-stars general" Günter Kießling pensioned, who was also vice-commanding officer of the NATO in Europe. That happened without giving any official reasons of the premature retirement. The Minister of Defence, Manfred Wörner (CDU), expressed himself on the affair Kießling during a cabinet meeting on 11 January. Wörner reported that there would be enough evidence of homosexual contacts of Kießling and that he had been become a security risk therefore. The knowledge of the military counterintelligence (**M**ilitärischer **A**bschirm**D**ienst – **MAD**) turned out soon to be utmost questionable. After fierce criticism ordered Wörner the discontinuance of all investigations and initiated the rehabilitation of Kießling. The dubious clear-up methods of the MAD became the object of a fact-finding committee now.

The other affair, which shocked the people of West Germany, was the party donation scandal: On 15 March was for the first time the industrialist Friedrich Karl Flick heard by the fact-finding committee of the West German Parliament (Bundestag). Friedrich Karl Flick was owner of one of the biggest German economic empires. The job of the so-called Flick-committee was to investigate within the scope of the party donation affair the intervention of Flick's combine in politics and members of the government. This committee should also find out to what extent financial grants of the combine played a part. Then, on 29 August 1985, was started the "Party Donation Lawsuit" in Bonn. Now the West German authority was engaged in a lawsuit with the former ministers for economic affairs, Otto Graf/Count

Lambsdorff and Hans Friedrichs (they were members of the party FDP), and also with a former manager of the combine of Flick, Eberhard von Brauchitsch.

This year began by cable television and satellite transmission in German language a new media epoch. On 1 January of this year the first West German television stations started with their test programme by cable TV. The transmission of the programme was to be considerably expanded in the near future then. On 1 April followed another pilot project.

The broadcasting of TV-programmes by satellite happened up to now over the "European Communication Satellite" (ECS), because the realization of the German-French common project TV-SAT/TDF 1 was put off. The "Bundespost" (Federal Post of West Germany) rented two channels from Eutelsat, the running enterprise of ECS. The satellite TV, of which reception is only possible by means of special antennas, had the advantage over the conventional terrestrial broadcast technique by its greater range, by its better reception and the bigger number of programmes.

During this year began also the first private television stations to televise their TV-programme.

We write the year **1985**

On 1 February made a commando of the "**Rote Armee Fraktion**" (**RAF**) an attempt on Ernst Zimmermann's life. Ernst Zimmermann was chairman of the management of the company "**Motoren- und Turbinen-Union**" (**MTU**) and president of the "**Bundesverband der Deutschen LuftfahrtIndustrie**" (**BDLI** = Federation of the German Aircraft – and Astronautics Industry). Ernst Zimmermann died of the aftermath of the attempt on his life in the evening of the same day.

On 13 February was inaugurated the reconstructed opera house of Dresden, the famous "Semper Oper". The opening ceremony happened with the romantic opera "Der Freischütz" by Carl Maria von Weber. This opera by Carl Maria von Weber was the last opera, which was performed in the year of 1944; it was also the last opera before the destruction of the "Semper Oper" by bombs in the horror night of Dresden, February 13, 1945. Now the ceremony was considered by the political leadership of the DDR (East Germany) to be a cultural contribution to the strengthening of the own self-image after 40 years of the partition of Germany and to be a symbol of the peace intention of the **G**erman **D**emocratic **R**epublic (**GDR** = DDR/East Germany).

On 5 May visited the U.S.-American president Ronald Reagan together with chancellor Helmut Kohl the memorial place Bergen-Belsen and the soldiers' cemetery of Bitburg in the Eifel (-Mountains). The general public criticized the visit of the cemetery of Bitburg, because there are also buried members of the "Waffen-SS" (=Arms-SS, the special troop within Hitler's SS. -- **SS** = **S**aal-**S**chutz, the notorious troop of the Nazis).

On 8 May made the West German president Richard von Weizsäcker a speech that caused much attention. It was a speech on the occasion of the fortieth anniversary of the German capitulation, the end of the Second World War.

On 19 August went Hansjoachim Tiedge, who was the official in charge for the West German counterespionage and government director of the "Verfassungsschutz" (West German Office for the

Protection of the Constitution; this office was situated in Cologne), into the DDR. That was the beginning of a series of espionage's mishaps of West Germany.

On 10 December were the Nobel prizes awarded in Stockholm, the capital of Sweden. Since 22 years got a German physicist for the first time again this prize. The Nobel Prize winner was the director of the "Max-Planck-Institut für Festkörperphysik" (Max-Planck-Institute for Solid Physics) in Stuttgart, Klaus von Klitzing. Klitzing got the award for the development of the so-called Quantum-Hall-Effect (now: Klitzing-Effect). This effect makes possible to adjust the physical unit for electric resistance (Ohm/Georg Simon Ohm was a German physicist; he was born on 16 March 1789 in Erlangen, he died on 7 July 1854 in Munich. Ohm found the electric resistance out, Ω). The adjustment of the physical unit for electric resistance is done according to the "Klitzing-Effect" by means of a natural measure.

We write the year **1986**

On 31 January published the newspaper "Die Zeit" (Hamburg) an interview with the "Head of State and Party", Erich Honecker (East Germany). Honecker pleaded for more economic cooperation and for effective steps along the line noticeable disarmament in the middle of Europe. But he stressed also the independence of the DDR.

On 9 July committed the RAF a bomb attack again. Quite near Munich was the manager of the company Siemens, Karl Heinz Beckurts, and his driver, Eckhard Groppler, killed by a bomb. The police came to realize that there detonated a 50-kg-bomb by means of an electric device. Then on 10 October the next act of terrorism. The diplomat Gerold von Braunmühl was shot dead by two terrorists in front of his house in Ippendorf. One of the two arms was also used for the murder of Hanns-Martin Schleyer in 1977.

We write the year **1987**

On 29 January Mikhail S. Gorbachev, the head of the government of the Soviet Union, confirmed his reform line during a speech. The whole world took note of this speech, particularly since he had already initiated the new reforms on 25 February 1986. His advertised revolutionary reorganization roused the people all over to hope in the meantime that there will be a change in the socialism, that there will be a human social order in future, which could survive. Gorbachev connected the reorganization with his demands for "Glasnost" (the public) and "Perestroika" (reshuffle). That was to lead soon to the collapse of all communist governments in East Europe, too. This collapse also was to lead to the reunification of the two German states again.

At the end of January were also held elections for the „Bundestag"(Parliament of West Germany). The coalition of CDU/CSU and FDP achieved a success again; they had the majority although CDU and CSU had lost many votes. The winners of this election were FDP and "The Greens".

On 23 March Willy Brandt announced his premature resignation as head of the party SPD. The reason for this step was inner-partial quarrels over the appointment of the Greek woman Margarita Mathiopoulos, who was a non-party member, to the post of the press spokeswoman of the SPD. Brandt's successor became Hans-Jochen Vogel.

On 7 September visited Erich Honecker as first head of the DDR West Germany officially. During his five-day stay in West Germany he had many talks with politicians of the Federal Republic of Germany. He also visited his sister in Saarland; there he was also born.

This year shocked the affair about Uwe Barschel West Germany. On 25 September Uwe Barschel (CDU), who was Minister President of Schleswig-Holstein, had announced his resignation for October 2nd. By it he drew the conclusions from the so-called Pfeiffer-Affair. Reiner Pfeiffer, who was the former official informant of the "Staatskanzlei" (State Office) of Kiel (capital of Schleswig-Holstein) for the media, had heavily reproached the Minister President during an interview of the magazine "Der Spiegel" and caused by it the greatest political scandal in the history of West Germany. According to what Pfeiffer said Uwe Barschel had used dubious means during the last electoral battle in Schleswig-Holstein. The background was the bad chance of the CDU in the run-up to the election. The CDU, which got still 49% of the votes at the state election of 1983 in Schleswig-Holstein, was afraid of losing the power in view of the SPD, which became stronger under the leadership of Björn Engholm. So Barschel – what Pfeiffer said – tried consequently to slander Engholm by means of dragging him through the mud. By spying on him should get gathered compromising material with the intention of elimination an unpleasant political rival.

The affair about Barschel came to a dramatic head. Barschel was put more and more under pressure after his resignation. Now his own party (CDU) refused him even the support. Uwe Barschel couldn't any more contribute to clearing up of the affair. He was found, dead, on 11 October in a hotel of Geneva/Switzerland. His dead body was lying in a bathtub. Was it murder or suicide? This question could never get answered.

There was a very sad balance at the Berlin Wall. Up to now were 133 persons killed at this terror wall. But on the border between the two German states were killed even more, there shot the soldiers of the DDR more than 800 refugees dead and some thousand were arrested in

East Germany; it happened only because they had another political opinion, because they weren't convinced communists.

We write the year **1988**

On 17 January were 120 persons, who were opposed to the communist system, arrested by members of the "**Staa**tss**sicher**heitsdienst" (**Stasi** = State Security Service) of the DDR. That happened during the demonstration in East Berlin, which took place in memory of the murder of the communist leaders Rosa Luxemburg and Karl Liebknecht. These 120 dissidents wanted to demonstrate against the repression by the East German state.

There was a serious mine disaster on 1 June in West Germany. In Borken were 57 "kumpels" (= miners) buried alive. 65 hours after the disaster were 6 kumpels saved, but the other miners died deep down in the mine.

On 28 August shocked another catastrophe the people of West Germany. During a show of fighter planes on the U.S.-American air force base in Ramstein (place in the Palatinate) three fighters collided in the air. The burning parts of the wrecked fighters fell from the sky and killed 70 persons. Some hundred persons were injured. In West Germany that was the greatest catastrophe of the years after the last war.

On 11 November Philipp Jenninger, a member of the CDU, announced his resignation from the post as "Bundestagspräsident" (President/Speaker of the Bundestag/West German Parliament). By it he drew the conclusions from the row, which was caused by his commemorative address in parliament for the fiftieth anniversary of the Jew's pogroms of 9 November 1938. Jenninger's address was vehemently criticized because of numerous misleading and non-sensitive wordings, what everybody could understand as justification of the pogroms.

A hostage drama kept for day and days the people of West Germany in suspense in this year. This drama began by a holdup. The Deutsche Bank in Gladbeck (a little town in North Rhine-Westphalia) was held up on 16 August. The police surrounded the building. The bank robbers, Dieter Degowski and Hans-Jürgen Rösner, entrenched themselves in the bank, took hostages and demanded cash and an escape car. The police yielded and made available this escape car. The bank robbers could escape and changed several times the car while fleeing. Then they captured a bus. During a stop they shot dead a hostage, who was just 15 years old.

After the release of some other hostages rode the robbers with two hostages into the centre of Cologne, there it was coming to macabre scenes now. The bank robbers had trouble forcing their way through the mass of reporters, photographers and cameramen. Whilst they were giving willingly interviews, they threatened their hostages to kill them.

On the autobahn (freeway) from Cologne to Frankfurt the police decided to go into action. The police officers rammed the car of the bank robbers by an own armoured car and fired off dazzling garnets. Another hostage, just 18 years old, died in the hail of bullets. But then the two bank robbers were eventually apprehended after the horror of an exchange of shots on the autobahn. These were scenes such as in a criminal movie.

The Minister Presidents (heads of the government) of the German Democratic Republic   -   (DDR/East Germany)

Otto Grotewohl	1949 - 1964
Willi Stoph	1964 - 1973
Horst Sindermann	1973 - 1976
Willi Stoph	1976 - 1989
Hans Modrow	1989 - 1990
Lothar de Maizière	1990

The reunification

We write the year **1989**

Within a few months the cemented post-war system, which existed for more than 40 years, vanished into thin air. In Germany the Berlin Wall, the symbol of the German partition, fell and in Europe broke the Iron Curtain. The people of East Europe had struggled for freedom and democracy; they had made great sacrifices for that.

In Germany there was not only the Berlin Wall that divided one nation, but also the death strip. What no one knew but many suspected, under the no man's land, the so-called death strip, there were loopholes for GDR spies. These holes were made of large concrete pipes and were hidden in wooded areas in which people hardly went. On Western side these pipes still ended on GDR territory. On this side was namely still a strip of 50 meters wide from the barbed wire, which belonged to the territory of the GDR (DDR). This strip could not be accessed by western border officials. GDR border guards observed both sides of the border strip, especially there where the loopholes were that only they knew. Only after the reunification also West Germany officially learned of these loopholes for spies. Today you can find them in certain places on the former death border deep in the forest.

The 7 January of this year was the first West German theatre day in the Soviet Union. In Moscow were for the first time West German stage plays performed. This was a sign of a change towards democracy in the Soviet Union, what was made possible by Gorbachev. The first sign of a political change followed in Hungary then. Hungary, a reform-oriented country, broke through the Iron Curtain as first communist state in East Europe and took down its boundary installation, which was installed to protect the communist system against Austria and the West. By taking down the boundary installation, a boundary of barbed wire and watchtowers with sharpshooters like the border between the two German states, the best-watched frontier of Europe fell on May 2nd. By Hungary's taking down of the boundary installation, was also brought about a new escape route for citizens of the DDR. The Communist Party of Hungary and the Hungarian government had started a definitive reorganization of their political system, which went more on than in other European countries. On 11 February of this year followed already the decision for a multiparty system a resolution of the Communist Party of Hungary of 23rd May 1988 for far-reaching national reforms, which designated the filling of the executive committee of the (communist) party with reformatory politicians. -- Since July of this year were more and more citizens of the DDR seeking refuge with the embassy of West Germany in Budapest (capital of Hungary). In August set in a stream of refugees, which didn't have an end, over the "Green Border" between Austria and Hungary. On 11 September, at O o'clock, permitted the government of Hungary the citizens of the DDR, who were in Hungary, to leave its country. That happened in view of the situation of the refugees and after the talks of the Hungarian Foreign Minister, Gyula Horn, with the government of West Germany. So came 57,000 citizens of the DDR via Austria to West Germany. It was a mass exodus. Some months later left Hungary the Eastern bloc as democratic state.

On 24 August also the political reorganization in Poland happened. The members of the Polish parliament (Sejm) elected Tadeusz Mazowiecki, who was the candidate of the "political arm" of the labour union "Solidarity", head of the government by 378 of 423 votes. He was the first non-communist head of government of an East European state. On June 4th and 18th of this year the "Civil Committee Solidarity" had already got the majority of votes during the first free parliamentary elections after the Second War in Poland.

This year also the political reorganization in the Soviet Union happened. On May 26th was held the first free elections for the last 70 years there. The citizens of the Soviet Union could elect amongst several candidates to the "Congress of People's Deputies" (Parliament of the Soviet Union). The reformatory politicians won this election. It was a great success for them. The orthodox communists suffered an election defeat.

At the end of this year also the political reorganization happened in Czechoslovakia and Romania. Whilst Czechoslovakia converted from a communist state into a democratic state without bloodshed, a bloody revolution occurred in Romania. This revolution took only one week, but more than 5,000 persons were killed.

Since August were more and more East Germans on the run; that happened via foreign embassies. The situation in the West German embassies in Prague (Czechoslovakia) and Warsaw (Poland) had dramatically come to a head in September. The citizens of the DDR had sought refuge by the thousand in the West German embassy in Prague. Previously they had to climb over the fence of the garden of the embassy there. In the garden was provided shelter for them in scanty tents. On 30 September brought the West German Foreign Minister, Hans-Dietrich Genscher, a positive message to the refugees of East Germany (DDR), they could leave Czechoslovakia, they could go to West Germany. The refugees in the garden of the West German embassy in Prague shouted for joy. Previously the governments of East Germany and Czechoslovakia had discussed about the situation within the terrain of the West German embassy in Prague. But then the East Germans had suddenly given the refugees permission to leave the West German embassy in Prague. But they could only leave Czechoslovakia by special trains of the "Reichsbahn" (Railway Company of the DDR) via German Democratic Republic (East Germany). Thus more than 6,000 persons (refugees from the GDR/DDR) came from Prague to West Germany.

Then, on 18 October, Erich Honecker resigned his post as secretary of the SED (Socialist Party) He said that he did it for health reasons, but really he did it under the pressure of the leaving wave of people and the so-called "Leipziger Montagsdemonstrationen" (Monday's Demonstrations of Leipzig). His successor to the secretary of the SED became Egon Krenz, who took also over the post as "Staatsratsvorsitzender" (Head of the State Council = head of the state) on 24 October.

On 7 October the DDR had still commemorated the 40th anniversary of the foundation of the German Democratic Republic. Amongst the 4,000 guests, who were invited by the East German government, was also Mikhail Gorbachev, the head of the Communist Party of the Soviet Union. Gorbachev gave a speech and pleaded for political and economic reforms. Honecker answered by a praise hymn to the achievement of the socialism in the DDR, but the momentary crisis he didn't mention.

Egon Krenz tried to save what was to save, but the decision to elect him as successor of Erich Honecker was met with disappointment by the East German population, because he was counted amongst the political hardliners of the SED. He was also a former head of the **FDJ** (Frei-Deutsche Jugend/Free-German Youth = a communist youth organization of East Germany) Egon Krenz was especially incriminated by the cheat at the election of May7th of this year and stood up for the massacre of June 4th of this year in Peking (China). But Egon Krenz also endeavoured to make reforms and showed readiness to carry on a dialogue after his assuming office.

Then, on 4 November, more than one million people demanded free election, freedom of opinion, abolition of the power monopoly of the socialist party SED, resignation of the communist government and admission of opposition parties, during the greatest rally in the history of the DDR. This rally took place in the square "Alexanderplatz" of East Berlin. The television of the DDR telecast this rally for three hours. This rally showed in plain terms that the citizens of the DDR had overcome the atmosphere of the fear of political persecution and had demanded with full determination a reform of the political system. But the subject "reunification" wasn't taken up.

At the final rally gave many personages and also representatives of the opposition a speech, so Christa Wolf, Stefan Heym, Christoph Hein, Steffi Spira and the pastor Friedrich   Schorlemmer. Also some representatives of the communist system had their say. But the former head of the secret service of the DDR, Markus Wolf, and Günter Schabowski, another representative of the communist system, were prevented from going on speaking by boos and hail of cat-calls.

Günter Schabowski, who was the head of the party SED in East Berlin, announced casually the decision of the Ministerrat (cabinet council of East Germany) during a press conference on TV of the DDR, that all citizens of the DDR could leave the German

Democratic Republic, if they would wish it, so they could also go to West Berlin or West Germany. That happened on 9 November at 18:57 clock exactly. This news, the travelling freedom and then the fall of the Berlin Wall, that all fell like a bombshell in the world. An immense crowd of citizens of the DDR inundated the checkpoints on the border between West and East Berlin now.

November 9, 1989; at 7 pm

TV press conference of the Central Committee of the GDR. Günter Schabowski, East Berlin SED chief, reports on the meeting of the Central Committee: Private trips (to West Germany) can be applied without the presence of advance statutes." This was the signal for the fall of the Berlin Wall.

At 23:14 clock were opened the barriers in Berlin under the on-rush of the crowd. Thousands and thousands of citizens of the DDR streamed to West Berlin. They met with a reception of cheers and sekt (= sparkling wine) by the citizens of West Berlin. On the checkpoints, there happened moving scenes. Many persons flung their arms round stranger's neck with tears of joy in the eyes. After the people had made a night of it made the ruling mayor of West Berlin, Walter Momper (SPD), a speech and said: "Gestern Nacht war das deutsche Volk das glücklichste Volk auf der Welt" (Last night the Germans were the luckiest people of the world)

Egon Krenz could only stay at the top of the state 6 weeks after his assumption of power. When the abuse of power of the leadership of the SED (Socialist Party of East Germany) got more and more apparent, Egon Krenz resigned his post as leader of this party on 3 December. Also the other members of the "Politbüro" (leadership) of the SED resigned their post now. The new strong man of the SED became Gregor Gysi now. He was lawyer and had a clean record. On 13 November the "DDR-Volkskammer" (People's Chamber = parliament of East Germany) had already elected Hans Modrow, who was head of the SED in Dresden, as successor of Willi Stoph and thus as Minister President of the DDR.

On 11 September founded 30 dissidents of the DDR the reform movement "Neues Forum" already. That happened in Grünheide close to East Berlin. It was the first opposition group in the DDR (There were soon political opposition groups within the Protestant Church too). Bärbel Bohley and Jens Reich belonged to the founders of the "Neues Forum". On 2 October constituted itself the group "Demokratischer Aufbruch". This group was predominantly composed of representatives of the Protestant Church. Pastor Rainer Eppelmann belonged to the founding members of this group. The first foundation of a new political party happened then on 8 October. It was the (new) "**S**ozialdemokratische **P**artei **D**eutschland" (**SPD** of East Germany).

On 28 November presented the chancellor of West Germany, Helmut Kohl, a plan for the cooperation of the both German states; when all is said and done then there should be a reunification of East and West Germany. But for the first time it should be a confederation, then later a federal state.

On 4 December citizens in Leipzig and some other cities of the DDR forced their way into the offices of the district administrations of the former "**M**inisterium für **S**taatssicherheit" (**MfS** = Ministry for State Security) incensed. They wanted to prevent the taking away and destruction of files. By this action should get secured that employees of the Stasi, what was the most important instrument of suppression of the DDR-regime, could get prosecuted. Then, on 7 December, the participants of the so-called "runder Tisch" reached the agreement about the liquidation of the **Stasi** (**Sta**atssicherheitsdienst = State Security Service)

The "**runder Tisch**" (round table): at the invitation of the Catholic and Protestant Church of the DDR came together representatives of the political leadership of the DDR and representatives of the opposition in proportional composition on 7 December. According to the example of Hungary and Poland the so-called "runder Tisch" wanted to work as controlling organ of the government till the planned election for the "Volkskammer" (parliament of the GDR/DDR) on 6 May 1990.

A photo from the year 2011, which shows a signboard, on which the following is noted: Here, in the course of the peaceful revolution in the GDR, the opening of the wall around the military restricted area "Brockenkuppe" (Montain peak of the Brocken, the highest mountain in the Harz Mountains) was forced on December 3, 1989 around 12.45 pm.

We write the year **1990**

On 15 November 1989 Mikhail Gorbachev (Soviet Union) had spoken about the reunification of Germany. That he did in front of students. The world heard that with surprise. Now the U.S.A. urged the Soviet Union to enter into negotiations about Germany's future. On 28 January of this year the United States presented their conception for talks about a possible reunification, the "Two-Plus-Four" package. West and East Germany (the "Two") should discuss the matter "reunification" with the four super powers (the "Four" = France, Great Britain, U.S.A. and the Soviet Union).

On 13 February, in Ottawa (Canada), they all agreed that Germany had to give up its eastern territories (= 25% of the whole German territory)   and that the German armed forces had to get limited to 370,000 soldiers. Also it wasn't allowed that troops of the NATO were stationed on the ground of the former DDR till the leaving of the last Soviet soldiers.

On 18 March was held the first, but also the last, free election in the DDR (GDR). The conservative "Allianz für Deutschland" won the election with 48% of the votes. The strongest power within this alliance of three parties was the party CDU with 40.6% of the votes. The SPD fell short of expectations; only 21.8% of the voters had given their vote to this party. The CDU, which has vehemently laid stress on a speedy reunification, met the opinion of the people of the DDR. The CDU also prevailed over the SPD at the elections of this year in four of five of the new German countries. The only exception was Brandenburg; there the SPD was the winner of the election.

On 5 May were started the "peace talks" with the goal of the reunification of the two German states. These talks, the so-called "Two-Plus-Four Talks", had the two German Foreign Ministers, Markus Meckel (East Germany, DDR) and Hans-Dietrich Genscher (West Germany), with the Foreign Ministers of the four victorious powers, Eduard Shevardnadze (Soviet Union), Douglas Hurd (Great Britain), James Baker (U.S.A.) and Roland Dumas (France).

On 1 July came into force a German-German treaty, which the two German states had arranged in the last weeks. By this treaty entered the two German states into an economic -, currency - and social welfare union. The DDR (German Democratic Republic) adopted the West German currency (DM-West). – The "Deutsche Bundesbank" of West Germany was the only central bank of the whole of Germany now. Wages, salaries, pensions, rents, leases and scholarships were calculated by a ratio of exchange of one to one (one DM-West = one DM-East). That happened although the DM-East had only the half value of the DM-West. But accounts of the citizens of the DDR were calculated only by a ratio of one to one for certain maximum   amounts. Children, who weren't older than 14 years, could exchange 2,000 DM-East in a ratio of one to one, persons, who were between 15 and 59 years old, could exchange 4,000 DM-East in this ratio and persons who were older than 59 years received 6,000 DM-West for 6,000 DM-East. All charges and liabilities, as debts of companies of the DDR, were mostly calculated in a ratio of two to one.

By the economic union was made the conditions to the DDR for a market economy: private property, a free price formation and freedom of trade were introduced, also it was made a new tax -, fiscal - and budgetary policy, which was adjusted to the market economy.

The DDR adopted within the scope of the social welfare union a pension scheme, health -, unemployment - and accident insurance. According to the example of West Germany should also get guaranteed the free collective bargaining, right to strike, the worker participation and the protection against unlawful dismissal   (= **Kündigungsschutz**)

Kündigungsschutz

The protection against unlawful dismissal is a rule by law; according to this rule is the possibility of dismissal of workers and employees (but also the termination of a tenancy agreement) restricted for social reasons. The employer can, if social reasons prevent him from pronouncing the dismissal, only reach his goal by a judgement. But then he also has to pay a severance pay often.

The DDR adopted over and above the essential environment rules of West Germany. A necessary "Generalüberholung" (complete overhaul) had to happen all over in the DDR, particularly measures for prevention of water pollution and air pollution control were needed.

Then, on 6 July, the West German minister of the interior, Wolfgang Schäuble, and the parliamentary permanent secretary of the Minister President of the DDR, Günther Krause, entered into negotiations for the reunification of the two German states. The political talks they had in East Berlin.

On 23 August the "Volkskammer" (People's Chamber = parliament of the DDR) had voted for the reunification with 294 votes against 62 votes. The condition for the German reunification was the "Unification Treaty", which was negotiated amongst the two German states. By this treaty was settled the fundamental internal questions of the union. But the adaptation of the right of abortion (DDR) remained open and required further clarification. Also the question of the capital (Bonn or Berlin) and the problematic nature of the ownership (there was no private ownership in the DDR, because that communist states didn't have normally) of landed property, which was expropriated after the year of 1949, remained still open and had to get settled later. Then, on 20 September, the "Bundestag" (West German Parliament) and the "Volkskammer" (East German Parliament) passed the "Treaty about the Reunification".

Previously, on 30 August, the governments in Bonn and East Berlin could still reach an agreement about the transitional period for the adaptation to the abortion law of East Germany (DDR). It was the last essential point of conflict amongst government and opposition of both of the two German states. Then, on 31 August, Krause (DDR) and Schäuble (West Germany) signed the treaty.

On 18 September the "Bundesverfassungsgericht" (Federal Constitutional Court of West Germany) still dismissed the action of eight politicians of the party CDU/CSU against the "Treaty of Reunification". These politicians had gone to the court because of the laying down of the line Oder-Neisse as final German frontier in the east. They wanted to prevent that Silesia, East Pomerania, the east part of Brandenburg, the little "Grenzmark" and the half of East Prussia with Danzig become Polish territories and the other half of East Prussia a Russian exclave under the new name Kaliningrad (the former Prussian city Königsberg). Memel (the land on the river Nemunas) should be a part of Lithuania now. The peace treaties, with the new German frontier, were still to follow in this year. Since this year (1990) was Germany thus smaller than before, it lost ancient territories, territories with German population and old German culture. Today there are still living many thousand Germans, but the vast majority are Polish people now or Russians in the exclave Kaliningrad. Landscape and towns have also new names there.

On 3 October took the reunification place. Many hundred thousands of Germans shouted for joy. (The October 3rd is the German national holiday today). "Sie (Wiedervereinigung) will nicht nur bezahlt, sondern auch gewollt sein" (the reunification must not get paid only, but must be also wished), were the words of farewell of the last Minister President of the DDR, Lothar de Maizière. The President of West Germany (now president of the whole of Germany), Richard von Weizsäcker, touched on the political side of the reunification: "Zum ersten Mal bilden wir Deutschen keinen Streitpunkt auf der europäischen Tagesordnung. Unsere Einheit wurde niemanden aufgezwungen, sondern friedlich vereinbart. Sie ist Teil eines gesamteuropäischen geschichtlichen Prozesses, der die Freiheit der Völker und eine neue Friedensordnung unseres Kontinents zum Ziel hat. Diesem Ziel wollen wir Deutsche dienen. Ihm ist unsere Einheit gewidmet" (It's the first time that we Germans aren't on the European agenda as point of issue. Our reunification wasn't forced upon anybody, but was peacefully arranged. This reunification is a part of a historical process of the whole of Europe, which aimed at the freedom of the nations and a new order of peace on our continent. We Germans want to serve this aim. Also our unity is giving its undivided attention to this aim)

On 3 October Germany also got back the last sovereignty, which it still didn't have, the air sovereignty over its country.

The heads of state of the two German states

Federal Republic of Germany (West Germany)

Theodor Heuss	1949 – 1959
Heinrich Lübke	1959 – 1969
Gustav Heinemann	1969 – 1974
Walter Scheel	1974 – 1979
Karl Carstens	1979 – 1984
Richard v. Weizsäcker	1984 – (1990)

German Democratic Republic (East Germany/DDR)

Wilhelm Pieck	1949 – 1960
Walter Ulbricht	1960 – 1973
Willi Stoph	1973 – 1976
Erich Honecker	1976 – 1989
Egon Krenz	1989

Germany with the new five German countries:

Country	Capital
Schleswig-Holstein	Kiel
Hamburg	Hamburg (City State)
Bremen	Bremen (City State)
Lower Saxony	Hannover
North Rhine-Westphalia	Düsseldorf
Hessen	Wiesbaden
Rhineland-Palatinate	Mainz
Bavaria	München (Munich)
Baden-Württemberg	Stuttgart
Saarland	Saarbrücken
Berlin	Berlin (City State and capital of Germany)

The new countries	Capital
Mecklenburg - West Pomerania	Schwerin
Saxe - Anhalt	Magdeburg
Brandenburg	Potsdam
Thuringia	Erfurt
Saxony	Dresden

Two famous German painters (and artistic performers) of the last years

Joseph Beuys

Joseph Beuys was born on 12 May 1921 in Krefeld; he died on 23 January 1986 in Düsseldorf. Beuys studied natural science and became pupil of E. Mataré after the Second World War. Since 1961 he was professor at the Academy of Art (Kunstakademie) of Düsseldorf, but 1973 he was dismissed because of a lawsuit with him. - 1971 he founded the "Organization for direct Democracy by Plebiscite" as following organization of the short-lived "Deutsche Studentenpartei" (Party of the German Students). Then, in 1974, he founded together with Heinrich Böll the "Freie Internationale Universität (FIU) für Kreativität und interdisziplinäre Forschung" (Free International University for Creativity and interdisciplinary Research) His social-utopian idea was to gain shape as "social plastic" by this foundation. Beuys staged many spectacular actions, so for example: "Wie man dem toten Hasen die Bilder erklärt", 1965 (as you explain the pictures to the dead hare; 1965); "Iphigenie/Titus Andronicus", 1969; "I like America and America likes me", 1974. By these actions he demonstrated with the urgency of a Shaman the moments of the menace of all human life. His objects are characterized by use of materials like fat, felt, honey, wax, chocolate and blood.

Beuys held the opinion that everybody is an artist. Beuys was the most successful German artist of the period after the Second World War. The museum Guggenheim in New York (U.S.A.) arranged for him as first living German artist since 1945 a work show.

Joseph Beuys

Jörg Immendorff

Jörg Immendorff was the most famous painter of Germany at the beginning of this century. He was born on 14 June 1945 in Bleckede on the Elbe (river). He studied at the Academy of Art in Düsseldorf; his masters were Joseph Beuys and Teo Otto. Immendorff became especially known by his 19 paintings of the cycle "Café Deutschland". This cycle described in a graphic and expressive style the reality in West Germany. Immendorff painted later the portrait of Chancellor Gerhard Schröder.

Jörg Immendorff was eleven years professor at the Academy of Art in Düsseldorf; he also died after a long illness in May 2007 there.

Jörg Immendorff

Germany in the last years of the 20th century

We write the year **1991**

During this year the Soviet Union disintegrated. Several new independent states came into being, so Estonia, Latvia, Lithuania, Byelorussia, the Ukraine, Moldavia, Georgia, Armenia, Azerbaijan, Turkmenistan, Uzbekistan, Tadzhikistan, Kyrgyzstan, Kazakhstan and Russia (a federal republic and the largest country of the world). Whilst the Soviet Union disintegrated the European Union came into being in the middle of Europe. Twelve heads of state and government of the European Community decided during the summit conference of Maastricht (town in the Netherlands), which was lasting till December 12th, to create a Union. The heart of the union should be an economic and monetary union till 1999. The basis of the monetary union should be the new European system of rate of exchange, which was adopted in the year of 1979 and had brought stable rates of exchange about amongst the states of the European Community. Latest in the year of 1999 the states, which could show a solid fiscal policy according to certain criteria of persistence of convergence and had stabilized the inflation on a low level, should adopt the European currency (EURO) as means of payment. Then, on 1 January 1994, was also created an independent European monetary institute, which should prepare the new European currency with the goal, this currency also to adopt till 1999 really.

On 1 April, in the evening, Detlev Karsten Rohwedder, the head of the "Berliner Treuhandanstalt", which was the competent authority for the administration of the national property of the former DDR, was killed by terrorists of the RAF. In his villa in Düsseldorf he was fatally injured by shots, which were fired through the window of the bedroom from an allotment garden, only 60 m away from his house. Then, on 13 April, Birgit Breuel became his successor to the office as head of the "Berliner Treu-handanstalt".

On 20 June the "Bundestag" (the German parliament) chose Berlin as the capital of the reunited Germany. It happened with (only) 338 against 320 votes. The preceding debate of more than 100 speakers was extreme controversial. Loser became the capital of West Germany, Bonn. In November the "Ältestenrat" (old-age councillors) of the German parliament reached the agreement that the "Bundestag" moved into the old building of the "Reichstag" (the former building of the parliament of the German Reich) close to "Brandenburg Gate". It preceded advertising actions, negotiations amongst the parties and public signature's actions with the narrow decision about the seat of government in future.

On 17 September the extreme right-wing violence escalated in Hoyerswerda, a district town in Saxony, after an assault on Vietnamese traders (former foreign workers from North Vietnam, who worked in the GDR/DDR) by neo-Nazis. In the following days young right-wing extremists attacked a hostel of foreigners and an accommodation of persons who were asking for political asylum. Every evening happened hunts on foreigners there.

On 19 September 400 members of the extreme right-wing scene threw fire things, stones and steel balls at a hostel of foreigners, in which living foreign workers from Mozambique and Vietnam. One day later were windows broken by stones, 17 persons were injured by it. The police arrested 24 rioters till 21 September, 70 occupants of the hostel were evacuated as a precaution. On 22 September the actions of violence directed themselves against the hostel of persons seeking asylum. 100 disguised persons attacked the building with petrol bombs and steel balls. There were 4 seriously injured persons and 28 persons with minor injuries. The applicants for asylum moved away, they got another accommodation. Politicians and media expressed themselves with concern that the population was apparently in sympathy with the extreme right-wing offenders of violence. Curious bystanders accompanied with cheers and racist slogans the attacks.

The most of the offenders of violence, who were hostile to foreigners, were young persons, not older than 21 years, persons who belonged to the skinhead scene. In those days Germany had 5,000 to 6,000 violent skinheads, half the skinheads was living in East Germany. They had hoped for a rapid prosperity and were disappointed; therefore they got susceptible to neo-Nazi slogans.

We write the year **1992**

In Yugoslavia, which had disintegrated like the Soviet Union, spread the war over the whole territory. On 25 June 1991 the Yugoslavian countries Slovenia and Croatia had declared their independence; Bosnia-Herzegovina and Macedonia were to follow. Thus Serbia-Montenegro formed the remainder of Yugoslavia. Whilst the Yugoslavian army tried in vain to prevent Slovenia from separating, this army tried it with all its might in Croatia now. But soon the Yugoslavian army also abandoned the attempt to prevent the independence of Croatia, because also Bosnia-Herzegovina aimed at separating. On 3 March Bosnia-Herzegovina also declared its independence. Since in Bosnia-Herzegovina were living ethnic groups, there were tensions and a civil war now. On 18 March the three ethnic groups of Bosnia-Herzegovina, Serbs, Croats and Bosnians (Moslems) came to an agreement: the country was subdivided into a federation with three territories. Then, on 6 April, the European Community recognized the country Bosnia-Herzegovina as independent state. In June the state authority of this country became non-functioning, because Serb separatists controlled 70% of the territory of Bosnia-Herzegovina. As result the UNO decided to send a peace troop to Bosnia-Herzegovina, also German soldiers went to this country so.

This year extreme right-wing violence against foreigners in Rostock and Mölln (towns in Mecklenburg-West Pomerania) shocked all people of Germany. In the time between 22 and 27 August right-wing extremists kicked up bad rows in Rostock. The excess developed into the worst demonstration of German anti-alien feeling since the unrest of Hoyerswerda (1991). The pictures ran around the world and impaired the reputation of Germany. – On 23 November right-wing extremists killed a Turkish woman (51 years old) and two children (girls, 10 and 14 years old) by an arson attack on town houses in Mölln. Some days later the offenders were arrested, it was a casual labourer (25 years old) and a trainee (19 years old); they belonged to an extreme right-wing group. Still the same day hundred thousand and hundred thousand people in Germany demonstrated against the anti-alien feeling. Then, in the following days, followed many rallies, the height formed a cordon of lights on 6 December in Munich. 400,000 persons demonstrated against intolerance and anti-alien feeling there.

This year also a new law on abortion passed through the German parliament. As we know, there was the possibility in the former DDR to have an abortion within the first 12 weeks of the pregnancy. Now the "Fristenlösung" (time limit for the abortion) was adopted in the whole of Germany, but that with compulsory consultation; that is, the women must have reasons for their abortion (illness or social reasons, which justify the abortion)

On 29 July Erich Honecker came back to Germany. He fled to Moscow in the year of 1991 and had asked for political asylum there. Now Russia had extradited him. Honecker was immediately arrested with his arrival in Berlin. It was taken legal proceedings against him because of murder (because of the murders on the border between the former two German states).

On 8 October died Willy Brandt, the first social-democratic chancellor of West Germany; he was 78 years old. The whole of Europe mourned for him, because he was a popular politician with the Europeans.

On 6 December a new regulation of the right of asylum followed in Germany. After a mammoth negotiation (50 hours), the ruling parties (CDU/CSU and FDP) reached an agreement with the opposition (SPD) about this new regulation. It had preceded a change in politics of the SPD. The plans were rejected by all organizations of the refugees in Germany.

The number of persons, who sought refuge in Germany, had reached the highest level since 1990, 438,000 refugees came to Germany this year. They came above all from regions of civil wars on the Balkan Peninsula and Romania. But Germany didn't have put up the most refugees. Sweden had put up more refugees in proportion to its number of inhabitants than Germany.

The former declaration in Article 16 of the German constitution survived according to the new right of asylum: "politisch Verfolgte genießen Asyl" (Germany gives asylum to victims of political persecution). But refugees, who came via another country of the European Community, didn't have a claim to asylum. The "Bundestag" (German parliament) stipulated, which states were to consider without political persecution. But deportations could get only carried out, if a German court of justice had "ernsthafte Zweifel" (serious doubts) that a state, from where the refugee came, was really without political persecution.

The new law of asylum came into force only 26 May 1993. One year later the number of refugee went down, now there were (only) 322,000 refugees.

We write the year **1993**

On 3 May Björn Engholm, who was chairman of the SPD and Minister President of Schleswig-Holstein, announced his retirement from all political offices. He drew by it the conclusions from the fact, which became known, that he has given a wrong evidence for the so-called "Barschel-Affäre" in presence of the parliamentary fact-finding committee.

This year also an attempt on the life of foreigners became a dominating topic of discussion in Germany. On 29 May two Turkish women and three Turkish children (girls; 4, 9 and 12 years old) lost their life by an arson attack on their house in Solingen (North Rhine-Westphalia). The offenders, right-wing extremists, had fired the staircase of the old half-timbered house in the night.

On 27 June two persons lost their life with the arrest of presumed members of the terrorist organization "**R**ed **A**rmy **F**action" (**RAF**/**R**ote-**A**rmee-Fraktion). The carried out action of the special troop GSG 9 was very criticized because of numerous mishaps. Rudolf Seiters (CDU), the minister of the interior of Germany, took on therefore the political responsibility for these mishaps by his resignation on 4 July. On 6 May Günther Krause (CDU), one of the most distinguished politicians of the new German countries, had already announced his resignation. He was Minister of Transport in Germany. The chancellor, Helmut Kohl, wasn't willing to hold him longer in his position in view of series of affairs. Günther Krause came from Mecklenburg-West Pomerania.

We write the year 1994

This year the Germans were requested to come to 19 elections; this was an electoral marathon. In Lower Saxony the SPD achieved a great success; with the election of March 13 the SPD under the leadership of Gerhard Schröder, who was Minister President of this country, received 81 of 161 parliamentary seats. Thus this party had the absolute majority of the mandates. The CDU lost many votes under its leading candidate Christian Wulff and had to take the worst result (only 36.4% of the votes) since 1963. – There were still other elections in Saxony-Anhalt (June 26th), Saxony and Brandenburg (September 11th), Bavaria (September 25th), Thuringia, Saarland and Mecklenburg-West Pomerania (October 16th).

On 23 May the "Bundesversammlung" (= 1,324 electors = all members of the German parliament + persons of various social groups of the whole of Germany) had elected the new German President. It was Roman Herzog (CDU). He was 60 years old and president of the "Bundesverfassungsgericht" (constitutional court of Germany). Now he became successor of Richard von Weizsäcker (CDU).

On 31 August the last Russian troops left East Germany (the former DDR). Also Boris Nikolayevich Yeltsin, the President of Russia, was present at the ceremonious withdrawal of his troops. On 8 September also the last occupying forces of the West Allies left West Berlin, present were the French President (François Mitterrand), the Prime Minister of Great Britain (John Major) and the Secretary of State (U.S.A., Warren Christopher).

On 16 October was held the election for the "Bundestag" (German parliament). Chancellor Helmut Kohl and his party (CDU) lost 6.4% of the votes, but he could continue governing. Now the governing parties CDU/CSU and FDP had a lead of only 10 mandates on the SPD, Bündnis 90/Die Grünen (the new Green Party since 1990) and the new party **PDS** (**P**artei des **D**emokratischen **S**ozialismus, the successor party of the SED of the former DDR/GDR). The governing parties had before a lead of 134 mandates.

We write the year **1995**

This year dominated the discussion on the power struggle within the SPD the whole of Germany. On 16 November, at the party conference of the SPD, Oskar Lafontaine, the Minister President of Saarland, prevailed against the party leader Rudolf Scharping by a struggle ballot. Now Oskar Lafontaine became party leader of the SPD. Scharping was voted out of office because of lasting dealings in the party leadership, which were lasting for months, and because of increasing annoyance of the grassroots of the party at the style of leadership of Rudolf Scharping.

We write the year 1996

This year was made the first cut into the social net of the Federal Republic of Germany. The government wanted to make the manpower cheaper, to cut the state subsidy for the "Bundesanstalt für Arbeit" (Central Job Centre of the Federal Republic of Germany) and to reduce the expenses of the health insurance companies and the state pension scheme. On 1 October the reduction of the statutory sick pay to the employees was already applied, also the protection against unlawful dismissal was restricted. That was the beginning of the so-called "Sozialabbau" (dismantling of the welfare state). **Statutory sick pay**: The employees received in case of illness only 80% of their gross wages for 6 weeks instead of 100% before. Payment for overtime was left out of account now. **Protection against unlawful dismissal**: The law on protection against unlawful dismissal was in force only for companies with more than 9 employees now, before for companies with 5 and more. The government hoped that small enterprises would easily take on labourers on this condition. **Health insurance**: The financial grant for dentures for the insured of the 1979 and younger age group was cancelled. The sick pay of the health insurance, which was paid after the statutory sick pay of the employer, was reduced from 80% to 70% of the gross pay. The payable contribution for medicines was increased. **Courses of treatment**: The regular duration of cures was cut short from 4 to 3 weeks; granted was a cure only every 4 years, up to now it was every 3 years. Two days' holiday each week of cure were subtracted. The extra pay of the insured was increased. **Job-seeker's allowance**: The adaptation of the unemployment benefit to the development of the wages was cancelled for the year of 1997; this also applies to the state maintenance payment and old-age transitional payment. The level of the expenses of the "Bundesanstalt für Arbeit" (Central Job Centre of Germany) in the new countries (East Germany) should get adapted for job-creation measures, for education and training to the level of West Germany till 2000, i.e., the level should lower.

The great social and economic topic of this year was, apart from the unemployment, the discussion on the economic measures of the government. The big cuts' package, the dismantling of the welfare state (Sozialabbau), was laid down by law by the majority of the parties CDU/CSU and FDP on June 28th. 4.3 million persons were unemployed at this time. Germany had never before so many people without job after the Second World War. The responsible persons in politics, in economy and in the labour unions were looking for a way out this crisis. During a summit meeting of the German government and the parties to a wage agreement on January 23, a platform for a "Bündnis für Arbeit" (alliance for jobs) was already passed; the labour unions were willing for going easy on wage claims and for another flexibility of the working hours to create 2 million new jobs. The employers agreed in principle to the reduction of overtimes. But the alliance for jobs didn't come off after the cuts' package of the government.

The countries Berlin and Brandenburg should get united into one country. 53.4% of the voters of Berlin voted for the uniting of the two countries, but in Brandenburg voted 62.7% against this uniting. The fusion, which was decided by the parliaments of

Berlin and Brandenburg in June 1995, failed with it. Berlin and Brandenburg remained separate countries.

On 11 April there was a catastrophe at the airport of Düsseldorf, the biggest charter airport of Germany. By welding works at an access a fire broke out. There was no fire guard although the direction provided that. 17 persons died very painfully in the flames, 62 persons were seriously injured.

We write the year **1997**

This year there was a natural disaster in East Germany. The water of the Oder (Odra), the border river between Poland and Germany, increased after heavy rainfalls. The flood, which had reached the country Brandenburg on 17 July, broke through the first levee by Brieskow-Finkenheerd on 23 July. 100 metres of the protecting rampart was flushed away. On 27 July the water level in Frankfurt on the Oder had a historic altitude of 6.57 m. On 1 August was noted a gradual fall of the water level. Five days later the first people returned to their houses. 6,480 people were evacuated before. The fight against the water of the Oder, which was lasting more than 3 weeks, was the biggest duty in a disaster area since the last war in Germany. 45,000 helpers, amongst them 30,000 soldiers, were on duty.

On 26 April Roman Herzog (CDU), the German President, had made his first great speech in Berlin. It was Herzog's so-called "Berliner Rede". He reproached the élite of politics and economy with failure of urgent reforms: "Durch Deutschland muss ein Ruck gehen" (A jolt must go through Germany) he said in front of 200 invited guests. These were his famous words, words of historic importance.

We write the year 1998

On 3 June occurred the most serious train accident after the Second World War in Germany. The ICE 884 "Wilhelm Conrad Röntgen" (ICE = Inter-City-Express; these trains always bear names) couldn't keep the track by a technical defect. The back part of the train crashed at a high speed against a bridge close to the town Enschede in North Germany. The bridge broke down by it. More than 1,200 helpers tried to rescue the injured, but 101 persons lost their life, the help was too late. The whole of Germany mourned for the casualties. Nobody could understand, how that could happen, because the ICEs were the most modern trains of the world.

On 27 September were held parliamentary elections again. The Social Democrats (SPD) with their leading candidate Gerhard Schröder became the strongest power in the parliament and that for the second time. The SPD received 40.9% of the votes; the party "Bündnis 90/Die Grünen" received 6.7% of the votes. Now, these (two) parties (Red-Green) had more members in the parliament than the other parties together. With 21 mandates more "Red-Green" had the absolute majority in the "Bundestag".

SPD and Bündnis 90/Die Grünen agreed within 2 weeks on a coalition's treaty. The treaty, which was now showed, had the name: "Aufbruch und Erneuerung – Deutschlands Weg in das 21.

Jahrhundert" (Start and revival – Germany's way into the 21st century).

On 27 October Gerhard Schröder was elected chancellor of the Federal Republic of Germany by the "Bundestag". He was the seventh chancellor. 351 Members of Parliament voted for him and 287 Members against him. Whilst the "Greens" had already determined their ministers (Joschka Fischer = Foreign Minister, Jürgen Trittin = Minister of Environment and Andrea Fischer = Minister of Health), the election of the ministers of the SPD was suspense-packed to the very end. Rudolf Scharping, who was parliamentary party leader of the SPD, let appointed himself Minister of Defence only at Oskar Lafontaine's insistence. Oskar Lafontaine was the leader of the SPD. Jost Stollmann, who was a non-party businessman, should be Minister for Economic Affairs, but he retired surprisingly on 19 October. Now became Werner Müller "Minister for Economic Affairs". He was also a non-party businessman; he was on the Board of one of the biggest companies of Germany, the VEBA combine.

The new German government got into turbulence short time after the swearing-in. Jürgen Trittin, the new Minister of Environment, met with stiff opposition of the atom lobby because of his nuclear policy and Oskar Lafontaine gave up in March of the following year. He was disappointed at the new politics and became a private person now.

On 27 September Helmut Kohl (CDU) had to take leave of the post as chancellor, his party had too clearly lost the election. The "chancellor of the reunification" returned never again to the politics. He was a private person now and let celebrate himself as the great politician of post-war Germany.

This year was also held an election in Mecklenburg-West Pomerania. There also the SPD became the strongest power in the parliament. The SPD received 34.3% of the votes, whilst the CDU (only) received 30.2% and had lost many votes so. The PDS (the former Communist Party) received 24.4%. Five weeks later Mecklenburg-West Pomerania had the first SPD/PDS government of Germany. Previously the leading candidate of the SPD, Harald Ringstorff, had still a talk with the CDU. But the political differences were too great, so Harald Ringstorff decided on the PDS on 11 October and formed with this party the new government of Mecklenburg-West Pomerania.

We write the year **1999**

This year began a bad civil war on the Balkan Peninsula. Kosovo, a Serb province where the vast majority are Albanians, wants to part with Serbia. The UÇK, the Albanian liberation army, fought against the Serb army. But the Serbs couldn't defeat the Albanians, so began task forces of the Serbs with the murder and systematic expulsion of Albanians. That was the reason for the action of troops of the NATO now.

On 24 March at 20:00 o'clock the NATO started the air raids on marks in Kosovo and Serbia. The first phase of attack directed against the Yugoslav (Serb) air defence, radar, command centres, ordnance depots and ammunition depots. The air raids, 13 states took part in these raids, amongst them also the tactical aircraft of the German air force, were the attempt to stop the expulsion of the Albanian population from Kosovo and to stop the beginning genocide there, too.

On 10 June the Serb army withdrew from Kosovo and the recovery of this country began step by step. On 20 September the UÇK, the resistance army of Kosovo, consented to the own disbandment. But now there were the troops of the UNO (KFOR = Task Force for Kosovo)   with 50,000 soldiers, who had the job to pacify this country, a country with gigantic problems. Kosovo was divided into protective zones under the sovereignty of the following states: United States, Great Britain, France, Italy and Germany. Now the expelled Albanians came back in masses. They immediately took revenge on Serbs and Roma people (a tribe of the gypsies).   Since the KFOR had taken protective measures for the Serbs, these troops of the UNO also became a target of the aggressions of the Albanians.

On 1 January of this year was also introduced the new currency, the **EURO.** But that was no change for the Germans, because they had to pay by DM now as ever. Only the share prices were noted in EURO since January 4th (rate of exchange: 1.95583 DM for 1 EURO). But since 1 of one to one to the EURO, the ratio of exchange of the ECU to the US-Dollar had to be multiplied by the ratio of exchange of the national currencies to the US-Dollar only. On an electronic note board was showed the ratios of exchange now.

After a successful start on the foreign exchange market, the EURO weakened in the course of the year there. Its ration of exchange on the stock exchange of New York (in the Wall Street) dropped for the first time to a value under one US-Dollar on 2 December. The EURO had started with a value of 1.1789 US-Dollar in January. A strong US-American economy, the interest's difference between Europe and the United States and the politico-economic neglects in Europe were the reasons for the weakness of the EURO.

In May of the year of 1998 the heads of state and government of the European Union had finally given the starting shot for the European Currency Union (ECU), what was also the opting for the start of the EURO. Germany, France, Italy, the Netherlands, Belgium, Luxembourg, Spain, Portugal, Ireland, Austria and Finland had reached the quality criteria for the EURO, only Greece didn't reach them. Great Britain, Sweden and Denmark didn't want to take part in the ECU. Thus they didn't want to take part in the introduction of the EURO, too. It preceded a telephone conference of the governors of the banks of issue with the determining of the eleven invariable rates of exchange. The basis for the invariable rate of exchange amongst the eleven European states formed the respective market price of the US-Dollar. In Brussels found officials of the *European Commission* out in the meantime the rate of exchange of the *ECU* (the common currency value of the eleven currencies of the Euro zone, compared with the US-Dollar) Since the *ECU* (European Currency Union; ECU here = unit of exchange amongst the countries of the European Union) should get changed according to a former agreement in a ratio.

On 11 March Oskar Lafontaine, the minister of finance, had resigned his post. The reason was the fight for the political course within the SPD in favour of the chancellor, Gerhard Schröder. By the elections in Hessen, Saarland and Thuringia the SPD had to give up its government responsibility; in Brandenburg the SPD lost the absolute majority. By the austerity programme of Hans Eichel, who was the successor of Oskar Lafontaine, and the planned tax reform, the SPD gained ground again.

Gerhard Schröder also achieved a personal success. The big company of Philipp Holzmann, a building contractor, declared its insolvency. Gerhard Schröder intervened and could reach an agreement with creditor's banks of this company. For the company Philipp Holzmann, which was heavily indebted, was made a rehabilitation programme by the German government. Then, on 24 November, was signed the agreement for the rehabilitation in Frankfurt/Main.

This year was also elected a new President of Germany. The new President of the Federal Republic of Germany became the former Minister President of North Rhine-Westphalia, Johannes Rau (SPD). He was the new "father of the nation" like "Papa Heuss" many years ago. The election was held on 23 May in Berlin. Johannes Rau followed Roman Herzog (CDU) as head of state.

This year Germany had also a political scandal again. The former chancellor, Helmut Kohl (CDU), said that there exist so-called "black accounts". On these accounts would be registered donations, which were separated from the official accounts of statement. Therefore the German parliament set up a fact-finding committee on 2 December. Certified public accountants were put in charge of this case; they had to inspect the finances of the party CDU now. Other details came to light during the affair, so for example the existence of illegal accounts abroad, on these accounts were "parked" the funds of the CDU of Hessen. The CDU of Hessen wanted to finance the electoral battle by them in this country. Kohl's refusal to give the names of the donators drove his party (CDU) into an ordeal. Now Kohl resigned from the honorary post as chairman of the CDU after a request of the presiding committee of his party. That happened on 18 January of the following year. The report of the certified public account-ants, which was presented in January, couldn't clear up the origin of 12 million DM.

On 10 December Günter Grass, the famous German author of these days, received the literary Nobel Prize by the Swedish king, Carl XVI Gustaf.

Germany, a true partner in the world

We write the year **2000**

It's the beginning of a new millennium, Germany is a reputable country again, but there is trouble internally brewing. On 14 January the CDU of Hessen reported that there are secret accounts abroad. Some million DM were transfer to the "Landesverband" (Regional Union) of the CDU in Hessen and also to the CDU of Frankfurt/Main. On 18 January Helmut Kohl, the former chancellor, resigned from the honorary presidency of his party, the CDU. On 16 February followed Wolfgang Schäuble, who resigned from the post as leader of the CDU. Now the party CDU was urged to pay back 41,348,000 DM (into the national cashbox) because of its incorrect statement of accounts. Successor of Wolfgang Schäuble became Angela Merkel, the first woman as leader of this party. 96% of the voters of the CDU voted for her.

Also in the PDS, the successor party of the communist party SED of the former DDR, a transfer of power was in the air. On 7 April, during the first day of the party conference, a conference of three days, the party leader Lothar Bisky announced that he was no longer a candidate for the party leadership. The second bombshell was the doing of the leader of the parliamentary party, Gregor Gysi. Also he wanted to give up his post.

The "Bundeswehr" (German army) shall to become a new face. On 23 May the German Minister of Defence, Rudolf Scharping, presented his reformatory plans. He planned to reduce the forces till 2006 and to reduce the time of military service from ten to nine months. On 27 October was abrogated the law "prohibition for women to do military service with arms".

On 15 June the government and the energy industry reached an agreement after protracted negotiations about the opting out of nuclear energy. That happened during a nocturnal top-level talk. The 19 German nuclear power stations should get phased out. Then, in the year of 2015, Germany shall have no nuclear power station.

This year the petrol price went beyond 2 DM for the first time. Because there was also a price increase in the other European countries, many Europeans protested against this increase in the cities. The German government reacted to the price increase by a package of supports for the car's drivers.

This year the Germans were shocked by a disease of the cows, **BSE** (**B**ovine **S**pongiform **E**ncephalopathy or mad cow disease). The first time a young cow died of this disease. This cow was born in Germany. In a German farm, where was diagnosed this disease for the first time, 160 cows had to die now; they were slaughtered. How could infect a cow with this disease? Nobody knew that.

The first case of BSE in Germany let collapse the beef market here. Chancellor Gerhard Schröder (SPD) immediately announced a prohibition of feeding of animal meal. Protein, which has pathologically changed, was considered to be the creator of BSE. The low-price pet food for cows was made of slaughtering offal (80%) and animal bodies (20%). Now this animal meal must be replaced by plant protein.

Bundestag (Lower House of the German parliament) and Bundesrat (Upper House of the Federal Parliament) decided in double quick time to prohibit the feeding of animal meal by law. This law was put into force on 2 December. Then, on 6 December, it became duty that meat stock with an age of more than 30 months has to be examined by a veterinary surgeon. By this examination went 1 kg beef up in price, now the buyer had to pay 30 pfennig (penny) more.

We write the year **2001**

At the height of the BSE crisis, the health minister, Andrea Fischer (Die Grünen/the Greens) and the minister for agriculture, Karl-Heinz Funke (SPD), resigned. Now began a "ride on the merry-go-round" for ministers. Chancellor Gerhard Schröder laid stress on a new agricultural policy by the renaming of the ministry for agriculture (now: Bundesministerium für Verbraucherschutz, Ernährung und Landwirtschaft/Ministry for Consumer Protection, Feeding and Agriculture) and the appointment of Renate Künast to head of this ministry. The new department had a responsibility with regard to food safety and consumer protection, which was the responsibility of the Ministry of Economy and the Ministry of Health up to now. Ulla Schmidt took the Ministry of Health over (without the responsibility for consumer protection).

Hannelore Kohl, the wife of the former chancellor Helmut Kohl, committed suicide this year in her house in Ludwigshafen-Oggersheim. She was suffering from an incurable disease. She was allergic to light, so that she could only leave her house in the night.

This year women took up their duties in the armed forces of Germany for the first time. 244 young women - 151 in the army, 76 in the air force and 17 in the navy - started their basic training in the German "Bundeswehr". Then, in the middle of this year,

705 women already took over their duties in the forces. On 2 July also the first 227 women had taken up their activity as officer cadets.

Women could be on duty only in the military music corps or as first-aid woman up to now. That was changing by a judgement of the European Court of Justice. Now woman could be on military duty with arms according to this judgement of 11 January 2000, because that answers the principle of equality. That was the reason that the Bundestag abrogated the law against the military service of women on 27 October 2000. Now women had the possibility to be voluntary soldiers, it should be a service without liability.

Women and men pass through the same programme during their training. Also the dress is same for men and women. But the underwear the women have to buy on their own, they get "dress money" for it.

An incident, which shocked the world on 11 September, was the assault on the World Trade Centre in New York and on the Department of Defence in Washington. Also the Germans were shocked at the disgraceful outrage of some Islamic men. Suicidal assassins went by air, by hijacked aeroplanes, towards their goals, the twin towers of the World Trade Centre in New York and the Pentagon in Washington. There they finished a horrible act; they flew into the twin towers and into the Pentagon, more than 3,000 persons died by this assassination. It was an act of Osama bin Laden and his terror organization Al-Qaida, a radical-Islamic group of fanatic Moslems. Osama bin Laden stayed in Afghanistan; there he had found the approval of the government. Not more than 4 weeks later the air forces of the U.S.A. and Great Britain flew towards Afghanistan. There they attacked the camps of the terror organization Al-Qaida. It was the beginning of the offensive "Enduring Freedom". But in Afghanistan were also attacked the public facility of the Taliban, the ruling organization, which came to bin Laden's defence and refused to extradite him. In Germany nobody believes that soon also German soldiers should be in Afghanistan.

Bin Laden and the 11 September 2001

Bin Laden was born between March 1957 and February 1958 in Riyadh, Saudi Arabia and on 2 May 2011 by an American special forces killed in Pakistan. He came from a wealthy Saudi family and supported the struggle of the Mujahedeen against the Soviets in Afghanistan. He was the founder of Al-Qaida, the terrorist organization that attacked on 11 September 2001 with hijacked passenger planes the World Trade Centre in New York. Al-Qaida had already earlier attacks, even in 1999 on the U.S. embassies in Dar Es Salaam and Nairobi.

We write the year **2002**

On 1 January the **EURO** became the legal tender to 306,000,000 people in Europe. Now in Belgium, Germany, Finland, France, Greece, Ireland, Italy, Luxembourg, the Netherlands, Austria, Portugal and Spain the people paid by EURO only. But now in some European overseas territories and in the little European states San Marino, Andorra, Monaco and Vatican was the EURO the official currency, too. Three states of the European Union didn't adopt the EURO as currency: Great Britain, Denmark and Sweden. In Germany the people could still pay by DM till February, 28th of this year. Then they could (only) exchange the DM for EURO. That happened by the German Central Bank.

On 2 March was started the greatest military offensive of the US-American army and Afghan troops against the Taliban in the east of Afghanistan. The "Operation Anaconda" was successfully finished by the American army on 13 March. Also German soldiers of the special troop "**K**ommando **S**pezial**K**räfte" (**KSK**) had taken part in this operation. It was also put into action laser-steered thermos-bombs during this operation. On 6 March two German soldiers lost their life by an accident in a blasting site of Kabul (capital of Afghanistan). Also three Danish soldiers were killed by this accident. That happened during a defusing of a SA 3 – defensive missile of Russian construction. This accident was the result of a lacking training of the soldiers.

On 11 April, 14 German tourists died by a terrorist attack in Tunisia. On the holiday island Djerba exploded a small lorry, which was full of propane, in front of a synagogue, an object of interest of Djerba. 19 tourists were killed. The detonation also destroyed the windows and the elaborated ceiling decoration of this oldest synagogue of Africa. German detectives investigated. They found out that the assassin was Niser bin Muhammad Nasar Nawar, who stayed in the year of 2000 in a training camp of Al-Qaida in Afghanistan. He had prepared this attack on a long-term basis. During the attack were 45 German tourists in or in front of the synagogue. Some Germans were seriously injured. Then, on 23 June, Al-Qaida confessed the attack.

On 26 April were 17 persons killed and 4 persons seriously injured by a person running amok in Erfurt (capital of Thuringia). The person, who was running amok, was a former schoolboy of the Johann-Gutenberg-Gymnasium (a grammar/high school). The culprit was expelled from school some months ago, short time before his final examination, because of forged certificates.

On 1 July a bad air crash occurred in the south of Germany. An air freighter and a Russian aeroplane for passengers collided over the Lake of Constance (Bodensee). All passengers and the pilots were killed. -- A Boing of the German parcel service DHL with two pilots on board, which was on the way from Berga-mo/Italy to Brussels/Belgium, and a Tupolev of the Russian Bashkir Airlines with 69 passengers, amongst them many children, which was on the way from Moscow/Russia to Barcelo-na/Spain, were the aeroplanes concerned. According to the information of the German "Bundesanstalt für Flugunfalluntersuchungen" (Institute for Air Crash Investigation) had functioned the automatic warning system of the two aeroplanes, which were on a collision course. The pilot of the aeroplane of the DHL had followed the request to a descent. The warning system of the Tupolev had had a request to an ascent flight, but the pilot ignored that, because he had repeatedly received the order by the Swiss air traffic control "Skyline", which was the competent authority for the air safety in the south-west of Germany, to descend; so the two aeroplanes flew towards each other instead of making way. The two aeroplanes collided and many people had to die. It was brought an action against the air traffic controller of Skyline, but before the beginning of the trial he was murdered by a father of the Russian children, who were killed by the air disaster.

This year East Germany had a flood disaster, the highest waters since 1945. This year was also a heavy quarrel in the FDP (Liberal Party). On 20 October Jürgen Möllemann, the former leader of this party, announced his resignation from all political posts. Möllemann had given rise to criticism because of the opaque financing of an Israel-critical election poster. On 2 December the executive committee of the FDP decided to expel Jürgen Möllemann. The new leader of the FDP, Guido Westerwelle, reproached Möllemann with intention of "removing the primary axis of the FDP by a solo", by that he had badly harmed the party.

Jürgen Möllemann,
former leader of the FDP in
North Rhine - Westphalia

We write the year **2003**

On 22 January the German chancellor Gerhard Schröder (SPD) and the French President Jacques Chirac paid tribute to the Elysée-Treaty, the goodwill treaty that was made on 22 January 1963 by France and (West) Germany. During the common

meeting of the "Bundestag" (German parliament) and the French National Assembly (Parliament), a meeting of two hours, Schröder and Chirac called to "breathe new breath" into the friendship of the two nations. They spoke even of a "Schicksalsgemeinschaft" (community of fate).

In Versailles there met 400 of the 603 German and 430 of the 577 French members of parliament. The meeting had given rise to criticism in Germany. The expenses for the meeting were the reason; but a "Paris Sause" (to go for living on the fat of the Land in Paris) was out of the question of the trip abroad, which cost 90,000 EURO and had to pay the taxpayer. That was at least the opinion of the "Bundesverwaltung" (administrative authority of Germany), because it was to say that the German members of parliament had done without overnight stay in France.

At the same also the members of the German "Bundesrat" (Upper House) and the French senate had a meeting in Paris. There was also the 80th consultation of the governments of the two nations, but this time in the form of a common council of the ministers. The two governments (France and Germany) agreed upon a "Ten-Points-Programme" for the extension of the cooperation. In future it should be a close coordination in all fields of politics, above all in the fields of foreign politics, security politics and defence policy. Also the legislation should be coordinated in future. Two "secretaries-general of German-French cooperation" should coordinate the cooperation, one of them in Berlin and one of them in Paris. Ministers of the two nations should take part with more intenseness in the discussion of the cabinet of the partner country. Also the periodical summit conferences (every 6 months) should be done by a German-French council of the ministers. It was also suggested a dual citizenship for Germans and the French. During this anniversary the governments of the two nations had politically moved together than hardly ever before in the last 40 years, the years of the "Erbfreundschaft" (hereditary friendship). Schröder and Chirac were in agreement with the rejection of a possible war against Iraq. --- Schröder had made public before the ceremoniousness that Germany as non-permanent member of the Security Council (UNO) would never agree to a war against Iraq, which shall force Iraq to disarm. France had veto power in the Security Council; by it France could prevent the Council from making a resolution that legitimized a war.

On 23 January was held a conference in the course of the ceremony of the German-French youth parliament in Berlin. Now there was also opened the new French embassy at the "Brandenburg Gate", the landmark of Berlin.

On 19 February was pronounced sentence of the first worldwide trial against responsible persons of the assassination of September 11th, 2001. (World Trade Centre, Pentagon). The "Oberlandesgericht von Hamburg" (Upper Superior Court of Hamburg) sentenced the Moroccan **Mounir al-Motassadeq**, because of aiding and abetting for murder in more than 3,000 cases and the membership of a terrorist uniting with facts of tried murder and grievous bodily harm, to maximum penalty of 15 years' imprisonment. The court considered it as proved that Mounir al-Motassadeq, who was 28 years old, had taken part in the preparation of the assassination in the U.S.A., also that he belonged to the terrorist cell of Mohammed Atta, who was the death pilot of New York (World Trade Centre) later. The indictment was especially based on the proof of transfers of the defendant into the U.S.A. for the death pilot; the indictment also based on the personal nearness of Motassadeq to the terrorist group of Mohammed Atta in Hamburg and Motassadeq's stay in a training camp of Al Qaida in Afghanistan. In the year of 2000 he has been there. --- During the 29 days of hearing Motassadeq, who was student of the University of Technology in Hamburg-Harburg, said over and over again that he pleads not guilty and that he didn't have known about the plan of attempt of the life of people in the U.S.A.

This year there was an intense heat in Germany; never before Germany had such a heat. For 23 days Germany had a heat wave of more than 30 degrees centigrade in the shade. In West Germany (in Karlsruhe and Sauerland) there was even a heat of more than 40 degrees centigrade in the shade. Since no rain fell in the months between April and August in the middle and south of Europe, there were bad forest fires in France, Portugal and Spain. Old people suffered from the heat in the whole of Europe, many of them died. The heat was also in the Bavarian Alps so intense that the last glacier of Germany, the glacier of the Zugspitze (the highest German mountain), threatened to disappear forever. Germany had first-hand experience of the consequences of the global warming.

On 5 June Germany had a politics' tragedy. Jürgen W. Möllemann, the former leading politician of the FDP (Liberal Party), died as skydiver. The cause of his fatal parachute jump was never cleared up.

Jürgen W. Möllemann was a passionate skydiver. That day he got on a plane with ten other skydivers; the aeroplane started from the airport of Marl-Loemühle in Westphalia. Möllemann left the plane in an altitude of 4,000 metres. In the altitude of 2,000 metres opened the main parachute as planned. But then, in the altitude of 1,500 metres, the parachute released itself suddenly and the reserve parachute didn't open. Möllemann fell into the death. The police ruled other fault out after intensive investigation. The question was left open, whether Möllemann sought to find the death by his jump from the sky or whether he was only a victim of an accident. The investigators didn't find a farewell letter. Politicians of all parties responded with dismay to the death of Möllemann.

Jürgen W. Möllemann got into bad trouble in the last months. His party, the FDP, had parted with him because of his anti-Israeli statement during the electoral battle of 2002 (as known). The "Bundestag" (German parliament) had lifted the immunity of the independent Member of Parliament only 15 minutes before his jump into the death. The public prosecutor's offices of Münster and Düsseldorf let search Möllemann's offices and private rooms in Germany, Luxembourg, Spain and Liechtenstein. It was carried out investigation concerning Möllemann, who was 57 years old, because of tax fraud, offence against the party law, cheat and infidelity.

We write the year **2004**

On 6 February Gerhard Schröder resigned from his post as chairman of the SPD. His successor became Franz Müntefering. Müntefering accepted the nomination with the words: "das schönste Amt neben Papst" (The best job next pope)

On 21 March was held a special party conference of the SPD and Müntefering met with 95.12% approval, which was the best approval since 1991.

On 23 May was elected a new president in Germany. Horst Köhler received already the majority at the first ballot; he got 604 of 1,204 votes. So he became the next President of the Federal Republic of Germany.

On 6 June was commemorated the D-Day in **Arromanches** (France). 17 states and thousands of veterans of the Second World War commemorated the 60th anniversary of D-Day, the disembarkation of the troops of the Allies in Normandy (France). Also a German chancellor took part for the first time in the commemoration of D-Day; it was Gerhard Schröder, who was a friend of the French president.

As we know, troops of the U.S.A., Great Britain, Canada, Australia and other countries had landed on several beaches of Normandy in the course of the operation "Overlord". By the invasion at the Channel coast began not only the freeing of France from the German occupying power, but also the opening of a second front against Nazi-Germany that had to fight in the east and west now and capitulated 11 months later. The French president Jacques Chirac designated the reconciliation to Germany as "without precedent" during his speech of Arromanches. Also he said that the unyielding enemies of the past construct together the present time now and that they look together ahead. That turns out there is no future in hatred, there is always a way for peace. – Gerhard Schröder confessed to the historical responsibility of the Germans, but he also said that he didn't represent "old Germany of those dark years". "Mein Land hat den Weg zurück in den Kreis der zivilisierten Völkergemeinschaft gefunden", were his last words. (My country found its way back to the civilized nations). Germany is a true partner of all free nations of the world.

Germany is still busy with a problem, the large number of un-employed persons. The Germans also dealt with the problem of a new law, the so-called "Hartz IV-Gesetz" (named after Hartz, an industrial boss, who had already worked out three social laws for the German government) -- The "Bundestag" approved of the summary of unemployment relief and social security, which belonged to "Arbeitslosengeld II" now (Unemployment Benefit II = unemployment benefit after the normal payment for jobless, after one or two years of unemployment according to the age and employment years). That "Hartz IV-Law" produced great annoyance, many people demonstrated against this law.

Opposition and government had come to the agreement on the summary of receivers of welfare payments (social security) who are fit for work, and long-term unemployed in one system. That happened to lower the supporting payments for long-term un-employed. The government held on its plan, also when tens of thousands of persons demonstrated every Monday in the streets. The people especially demonstrated in the eastern cit-ies of Germany to articulate their annoyance at the dismantling of the welfare state.

We write the year **2005**

On 19 April was elected a new pope in Rome. Joseph Cardinal Ratzinger, a German, became pope surprisingly. He was the suc-cessor of John Paul II. The Catholics of Germany shouted for joy.

March 1977

Joseph Ratzinger as professor of theology in Regensburg/Bavaria

Habemus papam – we have a pope: Joseph Ratzinger was elected pope after a conclave of only 24 hours. He was 78 years old and took up his office as successor of John Paul II, who died April, 2nd.

Ratzinger was born in Bavaria. Now he bears the name Benedict XVI. Before his election he belonged to the most influential theologian in Vatican, there he was prefect of the congregation of faith for many years and the most important confidant of John Paul II. All over the world the Catholics were glad about the swift decision of the cardinals – above all the enthusiasm of the Germans was great. Benedict XVI took officially up his office April, 24th; he got the insignias of the papal power (**Ring of Petrus, Pallium**) during a ceremonious divine service on the Peter's Square. In 1951 Ratzinger was ordained as a priest and lectured as professor on dogmatic theory and fundamental theology at some universities. In 1977 he was finally appointed archbishop and cardinal. Joseph   Ratzinger, now Benedict XVI, was a conservative pope, who wanted to continue the course of his predecessor; especially that he wanted to do in the matter of abortion and euthanasia, which are subjects for discussion in the world. These are points, which by the general public are controversially discussed. The emphasis of a clear Christian faith counts as his main concern, as well the fight against the estrangement of the Christianity in the western world.

On 22 May was elected a new parliament in North Rhine-Westphalia. The ruling party, the SPD, lost the election. After the defeat Gerhard Schröder (SPD), the chancellor, announced that he aimed at new election in Germany. Since the German parliament (Bundestag) didn't have the right of self-dissolution, there was only one possibility according to the constitutional law: The chancellor proposes a vote of confidence. If he loses the vote of confidence, then he would have to ask the president for the discharge from the post as chancellor. The president has to prepare new election then. But many lawyers dispute that it would be constitutional, if the chancellor brings tactically about a vote of confidence, even though he is in actual confidence of the majority of the parliament. Therefore Gerhard Schröder also said in plain terms during a sitting of parliament before the vote of confidence, that he doesn't expect the imperative confidence of the majority of the parliament, since he has realized "klar abweichende Positionierungen" (clearly differing interpretation of the situation) within the red-green coalition. After the election in North Rhine-Westphalia it had given plain announcement to cancel a part of "Agenda 2010", also some Members of Parliament of the own party (SPD) had threatened to go over to the new "Left Party". -- **Agenda 2010** that is the essential part of Schröder's social and labour market reform.

Gerhard Schröder

Franz Müntefering, the leader of the SPD and leader of the parliamentary party of the SPD, had invited the Members of Parliament of his party to abstain during the vote of confidence by name. 140 of 249 Members of Parliament of the SPD followed the invitation of Müntefering. Gerhard Schröder could so reach his goal, because the CDU/CSU and the FDP voted with "no", what was to be expected.

On 21 July the chancellor asked Horst Köhler, the President, to dissolve the Bundestag and to prepare new election for September, 18th. Horst Köhler announced during a televised address that also he didn't trust in a majority of the Members of Parliament for Schröder. But the German government had to be functioning in a time, in which Germany would be faced with great problems.

It was the third time that the German parliament (Bundestag) passed a motion of no confidence. As already reported, in 1972 the CDU/CSU had tried to bring down the chancellor of those days, Willy Brandt (SPD), by a vote of no confidence. But Willy Brandt could prevail against Rainer Barzel (CDU), the leader of the opposition, who got two votes less than the absolute majority. Then, in 1982, the second time passed a motion of no confidence. Helmut Kohl (CDU) had lost the vote, as wished, and made free the way for new election. Two months ago he had become chancellor by a constructive vote of no confidence. Now he wanted to have been certified by the voters the change of government.

On 18 September was held the new election for the Bundestag. The CDU/CSU became the strongest power by this advanced election, but the CDU/CSU was only ahead of the SPD by a bare majority. This majority was neither for the coalition with the

FDP, which was intended by the CDU/CSU, nor for the continuation of the red-green government enough. Gerhard Schröder, who was the chancellor up to now, as well as Angela Merkel, the boss's wife of the CDU, laid claim to the post as chancellor. Schröder saw as moral winner himself. He had been able to reduce "the margin of the CDU/CSU on the home stretch"; the CDU/CSU was in a great lead according to the public opinion poll, which had been preceded. The leader of the SPD, Franz Müntefering, announced in the "Willy-Brandt-Haus" (the central office of the SPD in Berlin): "Das Land will Gerhard Schröder als Bundeskanzler haben" (The country wants to have Gerhard Schröder as chancellor).

In the "Konrad-Adenauer-Haus" (the central office of the CDU in Berlin) were the members of the CDU in low spirits. When at18:30 o'clock (September, 18th) Angela Merkel was on camera together with Edmund Stoiber, the leader of the CSU in Bavaria, everybody could see her shock at the lost triumph. Merkel emphasized that the "Union" (=CDU/CSU) would be the strongest power in the German parliament (Bundestag) and that she will take the "government order with all her might".

The SPD as well as the "Union" lost many votes and reached together less than 70% of all votes during the election. It was the worst result at all for the CDU/CSU during an election in the Federal Republic of Germany; the SPD had to bear its worst result for 15 years. Winner was the FDP with the best result since 1990 (11.0%) and "**Die Linke**" (The new left party – the union of PDS, the former party of East Germany, and the new western party **WASG** = **W**ahlalternative **A**rbeit und **S**oziale **G**erechtigkeit, which was a splinter group of the SPD). For the SPD voted especially the women, the men voted more for the CDU/CSU. The

SPD also got the most votes of workers, employees and unemployed persons whilst the CDU/CSU got the most votes of the self-employed persons and the pensioners.

On 10 October, three weeks after the advanced election, the CDU/CSU came to an agreement with the SPD. Angela Merkel shall lead the "Grand Coalition". The CDU/CSU nominated 6 ministers (also the boss of the Kanzleramt/chancellor's office became a man of the CDU), the SPD nominated 8 ministers. So Gerhard Schröder had to go and Angela Merkel came, the first woman as chancellor of Germany.

Angela Merkel, the new chancellor of Germany

She was born on July 17, 1954 as Angela Dorothea Kasner in Hamburg. Her grandfather belonged to the Polish population group, which lived in the province of Poznań, which belonged to the German Empire. His family name was Kazmierczak. When he later moved to Berlin, he changed his name to Kasner. Angela Merkel's father already bore this name when he was born.

We write the year **2006**

In Berlin are living the most foreigners in Germany. There are over and over again acts of violence of young foreigners. On 30 March asked the Rütli-Schule (a "Hauptschule" in the district Berlin-Neukölln --- Hauptschule = extended elementary school, classes 5 – 9) by a dramatic letter for help the senate of Berlin for support in the resolution of the problem of violence. The situation in the Rütli-School was thrown out of joint. On 31 March there were for the first time policemen to security and order in front of the school, also were delegated welfare workers and psychologists for the support of the teachers there. The letter caused not only a discussion about the "Hauptschule", but also the discussion on the integration of immigrants, because at the "Rütli-Schule" were only 20% German pupils, but 80% schoolboys of immigrants' families.

The plan the Hessian minister of the interior (Volker Bouffier of the party CDU) presented on 14 March was rejected by most people. The foreigners should take an extensive test of knowledge and human value. The Bavarian government decided on 4 April, parents who didn't let take part their children in German lessons in the kindergarten (nursery school), had to pay a fine. That happened in connection with other measures for a better promotion of the German language for foreign children. The ministers of the interior of the German countries agreed on a united settlement of naturalization. That happened on 5 May. Foreigners, who wanted to become naturalized, had to attend a course in German and to finish a class of naturalization in future. Then they had to prove their acquired knowledge. On 20 April Ursula von der Leyen, the minister for family affairs (CDU), had presented together with the two great

Christian Churches a common "alliance for education" in view of the increased acts of violence at schools. The "alliance of education" should work out the basis of the "Werteerziehung" (value's education) in the parents' homes and the kindergartens.

On 21 May was created the basis for a new state on the Balkan Peninsula. It was Montenegro, which had broken with Serbia. Montenegro, this little country, was the last country of the former state Yugoslavia, which broke the connection with Serbia now. 55.5% of the inhabitants of Montenegro voted for an independent state, 44.5% voted against that. The independence was proclaimed by the parliament of Montenegro then on 3 June. Under the cheers of many curious bystanders was the new national flag hoisted and the new national anthem played. Montenegro has only 650,000 inhabitants, the capital is Podgorica.

The new German government got down to the realization of its great plans, the reform of federalism and the start in a reform of the Public Health Service. On 30 June made the "Bundestag" the way free for a reform of federalism. The German countries got more authority by an extensive modification of the constitution of the Federal Republic of Germany. But the countries also gave away a part of their codeterminations in "Bundesrat" (Upper House of the Federal Parliament).

On 26 March were held three elections in Germany. By the elections were strengthened the heads of government in office. In Baden-Württemberg was the CDU-FDP coalition, which was led by Günther Oettinger (CDU), confirmed, in Rhineland-Palatinate reached Kurt Beck (SPD), who was the Minister President of this country, the absolute majority and in Saxony-Anhalt remained the CDU under the leadership of Wolfgang Böhmer the strongest power in parliament. But because of missing majority he had to govern with the SPD; before he governed with the FDP, which had lost too many votes during this election.

On 10 April Kurt Beck also became party leader of the SPD. He was the successor of Matthias Platzeck, who had resigned from his post because of health reasons.

We write the year **2007**

This year is a great year for Germany; it is a true partner in the world. But this year is also a year of surprises, a year of demonstrations and murder.

This year was held a great summit conference of the 27 states of the European Union in Brussels. It was a great success of the German chancellor, Angela Merkel. By Angela Merkel was reached that Europe will get a new voting procedure till 2014 and a controlling function of the national parliaments to the EU-commission. In future Europe will have also elected a "European Council-President" and a "High Representative for foreign and security politics" instead of a Foreign Minister.

Germany has a big problem with Poland in spite of great successes. The future will soon show, whether the brothers Kaczyński speak really on behalf of the majority of the youth of Poland by their look back at the German war guilt. But the reconciliation to Poland needs also a special attention, many little steps and much sure instinct.

More than 16 years ago, on 14 November 1990, the German Foreign Minister of that time, Hans-Dietrich Genscher, and the

Foreign Minister of Poland, Krzysztof Skubiszewski, had made the German-Polish border treaty. Germany and Poland considered the hostility, which was lasting for centuries, fortunately closed now. The treaty should be a document of the reconciliation to Poland. But now only could few radicals amongst the expellees and an anti-German government of Poland destroy all hope of reconciliation.

The organization of the German expellees, "Preußische Treuhand", acted only and brought 22 actions against Poland. They went to the "European Court of Justice for human Rights" and demanded the return of their former property in the former eastern provinces of Germany or a payment as compensation. The German government dissociated itself from this demand, but the Minister President of Poland, Jaroslaw Kaczyński felt compelled to reproach the German government with "complete stubbornness". Now he aimed at a new Polish law, which confirmed the Polish right of possession of former German possession in the former German east provinces. The foreign minister of Poland, Anna Fotyga, demanded even more, German territories in Saxony, Brandenburg and West Pomerania. She had thought of Berlin, the German capital, by any chance!!?? By the border treaty of 1990 was fixed the Oder-Neisse-Line as German-Polish frontier for ever, but the question of the possibility of individual actions, like the action of the German organization "Preußische Treuhand", wasn't settled.

Anna Fotyga finally withdrew her demand and claimed a change of the neighbourhood's treaty of 1991 now. Germany should guarantee that Germans didn't have claim to former possession in the former German east provinces. Thus Poland had to pay Germans no compensation. But the German state had committed itself by it to pay compensations for the German expellees from the former German east territories. The German government wanted to evade that. Jaroslaw Kaczyński continued to kindle the resentments against the Germans and to have fear of them. He also found a reason for that soon. A German excursion's ship sailed astray by an error and was in (the new) Polish territorial waters. That was after Polish mind a violation of the frontier of Poland, although Poland belongs to the European Union and receives multimillion EURO from Germany via Brussels each year.

In June was held a summit conference of the **G**reat **8** industrial nations of the world (U.S.A., Canada, Great Britain, Japan, France, Italy, Russia and Germany) in East Germany. During this summit conference was demonstrated again. There were bloody demonstrations like the demonstrations during the other summit conferences in the last years. These demonstrations belonged to the worst riots for more than 20 years. In Rostock overshadowed brutal attacks the peaceful protest of tens of thousands of people against the **G-8**-summit conference of Heiligendamm (little town in Mecklenburg-West Pomerania). Disguised persons (the so-called "Autonomous") had four hours street fights with policemen, who took massive action against the violent rioters in downtown Rostock, the big German seaport at the seaside of the Baltic Sea. More than 1,000 persons were injured, amongst them 433 policemen (30 policemen were seriously injured) and 520 rioters. The rioters were not only Germans, there were also foreigners amongst them, so Bulgarians, Austrians, Japanese, Spaniards, Frenchmen and Russians.

The demonstrations were continued during the summit conference of the **"G 8"** in Heiligendamm. The critics of the globalization succeeded in reaching the border fence (security fence to the conference). But also disguised persons of the "autonomous group" took position there. After all appeared water cannons, were brought into action riot sticks and tear gas. Previously some thousand demonstrators succeeded in reaching a surprise coup: they marched in line for miles through the fields, so they could get past the police cordon and some demonstrators could reach the last fence before the conference venue and could block the access roads there. One demonstrator shouted for joy "Die Herrschenden der Welt sitzen da und sind vom Protest eingeschlossen" (The rulers of the world are sitting there; they are locked by the protest)

Now in Heiligendamm followed the biggest police operation in the history of the Federal Republic of Germany. In the fields policemen landed by helicopters, water cannons made free the ways, demonstrators were carried away.

The most demonstrators were, however, peaceful. But the inhabitants of Heiligendamm had no sense of security in view of the marching up crowd of people. "Man weiß ja nicht, ob sie friedlich sind oder alles kaputt machen", said an inhabitant of Heiligendamm (Nobody knows whether they are peaceful or smash up everything).

Also rallies at the airport of Rostock-Laage belonged to the strategy of the international protesters. "Wir wollen die Kräfte der Polizei auseinanderziehen und möglichst viele Beamte im Bereich Laage binden", said a speaker of the protesters. (We wanted to bind many policemen in the area of Laage).

The spirits amongst the 6,000 blockers wavered between joy and fear. Joy, because they had succeeded in reaching the fence

-- and fear, because the police as well as also disguised persons of the autonomous scene had taken their position.

The march of the demonstrators from the camp of the critics of the **G 8** in Reddelich through the fields to the security fence had taken two hours. "Wir gehen jeder Eskalation aus dem Weg, aber wir lassen uns nicht aufhalten" was announced over and over again through the megaphones. – We walk away from any escalation, but we cannot stop us. – When the police had put up a road block, the demonstrators turned off into a forest or marched through the fields -- the leaders of the demonstrators knew best their way around Heiligendamm.

"Wir stellen uns darauf ein, dass wir sehr, sehr lange hier bleiben", said an organizer (We prepare ourselves for staying a long, long time here) But the street fights in Rostock had an effect. So the demonstrators admonished one another: "Pass auf dich auf" (Take care of yourself)

In August was held a great conference of the "grand coalition" (CDU/CSU and SPD) in the palace Meseberg (East Germany). The most important topics were the questions "job market, minimum wage, low-wage sector, sharing of the employees, protection of climate and lack of qualified personnel".

On 15 August occurred an atrocious murder in Germany. In Duisburg (a big city in **North Rhine-Westphalia**) were 6 Italians executed by 70 shots in front of a pizzeria. The victims, who were between 16 and 38 years old, died in hail of bullets near the central station. They were sitting in two cars and had left the pizzeria a few minutes ago. In the pizzeria they had celebrated the birthday of one of the murdered persons (just 18 years old).

The bloody deed was the result of a quarrel amongst two families of the **mafia** of Calabria (South Italy).

5 victims were related with each other. Three men lived in Duisburg; two men came from San Luca (a town in Calabria/Italy) a few weeks ago. In Duisburg they had lived with their relatives. All of them had a connection to the pizzeria, as partner or employee. The young man, who was just 18 years old, came from Mülheim (a city on the Ruhr/river, North Rhine-Westphalia) and didn't belong to the family of the other murdered men; he was trainee in the pizzeria.

The trail of blood led to the "Ndrangheta", an arm of the mafia in Calabria, after the information of the Italian police. The police of Rome/Italy was safe to assume that it was a bloody feud of rivalling families. It was a piece of news for the Italian police that such an act of violence could happen in a foreign country. Italian officers were sent to Germany to help with the investigations there.

On 15 August were also killed Germans in Afghanistan. The victims were three German policemen; they were victims of an attack of the Taliban. The order of the killed policemen was, to protect the German embassy in Kabul, the capital of Afghanistan. The policemen were on the way to a shooting-range in the east of Kabul; there they wanted to go into training with their weapons. But before they had reached their goal suddenly detonated an explosive charge and killed them in the white car of the German embassy. The German army was on patrol since 2002 in Kabul. Would the German army have been the target of the Taliban, the attack hadn't had this effect. The wheel tank "Fuchs" of the German army offers more protection against attacks than a car of the embassy, which isn't armoured. Cars of the embassy can ward off small explosions, but they have no chance against antitank grenades.

The antitank grenade was operated by remote control. The radical-Islamic rebels who had many sympathizers in environs of the attack confessed to the attack. During the last ten months were already three Germans killed by the Taliban, two employees of the "Deutsch Welle" (German Radio) and one employee of the "World Hunger Aid". Only a few weeks later, three German soldiers were killed by a suicide. Then, two weeks later, two German civil engineers were kidnapped by the Taliban; one of them was shot dead short time after that.

Now Islamic terrorists also tried a bloody deed in Germany. But this bloody deed could be prevented by the arrest of three terrorists in September. These three terrorists had planned bomb attacks in Germany. The terrorists – two of the terrorists were Germans who had converted to the Islam and one of them was a Turk – were arrested in Sauerland (a region in North Rhine-Westphalia). Now it was also investigated concerning five other persons. The three arrested persons wanted to detonate explosive charges in front of some American offices in Germany. That should happen because of hatred for the U.S.A. So they wanted to kill many people.

12 barrels with 730 kilogramme hydrogen peroxide were the element for the planned attempt on the life of many persons. This quantity 730 kilogramme hydrogen peroxide had had a bigger explosive power than the explosive power of the bomb attacks, which happened already in Europe and which had killed several hundred persons. The **BKA** (**B**undes**K**riminal**A**mt/Federal Detective Office) and the special unit GSG 9 had the men, who belonged to the terrorist group "Islamic Jihad-Union", observed

for months. This group was in contact with El Qaida. The terrorists came from Baden-Württemberg, Hessen and Saarland. They were trained in the terrorist camp of North Pakistan and then observed for 6 months by 300 German security officers. In the middle of July the police even succeeded in exchanging the contents of the barrels for a strongly diluted solvent; thus an attempt hadn't had a disastrous effect.

At the end of September the German chancellor, Angela Merkel, saw the Dalai Lama in Berlin. That caused a violent protest of the Chinese, who cancelled all planned meetings with German politicians.

Angela Merkel started off on a journey through Africa in October. In South Africa she met **Nelson Mandela**, the former president of South Africa. Angela Merkel and the old man (he was 89 years old) seemed to get along well. Mandela joked with the photographers and Merkel gave a friendly smile. She seemed to be fascinated by the moments, in which she could speak with this old man, who was admired in the world. **"Es war für mich ein bewegender Moment, Nelson Mandela zu erleben und zu sprechen",** she said short time after the meeting (It was a moving moment to me to see Nelson Mandela and to talk with him)

It was a special wish of the German chancellor to see Mandela during her voyage of (only) four days through Africa. She had met him never before. During the period of the DDR (East Germany/there she was living during the communist time) she had already pursued his fate. This meeting with Mandela she considered as exceptional honour. Mandela's most important words during the talk were: "Peace in Africa, no violence. All conflicts in Africa – in Sudan, in Congo or Somalia – must get resolved without violence". That was his main message. He said that he hadn't seen that so all the time before, but during his long imprisonment he had made a maxim from that.

In October were announced the names of the Nobel prize winners of this year. Also a German physicist from Jülich (little town in the region of the Lower Rhine/North Rhine-Westphalia) belonged to the winners. It was Peter Grünberg. His invention (also an invention of his French colleague Albert Fert) was the small hard disk of the computers of today. "We reward Peter Grünberg for his invention, which made possible to reduce the size of computers dramatically. You have only a close look at the monster of the year of 1964", commented the head of the Nobel Committee, Per Carlson, on Grünberg's invention. Stuart Parkin, a boss of the computer giant **IBM**, paved the way for Grünberg's invention in the year of 1997 and the new small hard disk could start its road to success.

The information is installed in the form of magnetic switch levers in hard disks of computers, MP3-players or digital cameras. These so-called bits can be switched on or switched off. The **IT bits** were compressed more and more in view of the upward tendency of the data flood. So the censors of the hard disk must especially well look to decode such data really; they are very compact on the disk. But now the IT memory capacity could be increased thirtyfold by the high sensitive Sandwich censors. Hard disks, which you can buy on the market today, have IT memory capacity of 500 Gigabyte. By this capacity you can IT save more than 500,000,000,000 letters on the hard disk.

The company **IBM** produced hard disks with the new technique for the first time in the year of 1997. Today this new technique is used all over the world and is in all hard disks of the last years.

This year Germany had still another Nobel Prize winner, it was Gerhard Ertl. He was also informed about this high award in October. Gerhard Ertl got this award for chemistry. He was honoured "for his studies on chemical processes on hard surfaces".

The awarding of the Nobel Prize to two German scientists had caused a great enthusiasm amongst all scientists and also amongst many politicians. Now the people were talking about an "atmosphere of start and the international status of the German research". Ertl and Grünberg praised the working conditions in Germany. They couldn't understand that many German top scientists emigrated and looked for fortune in other countries.

Angela Merkel, the German chancellor and great partner in the world, went to India at the end of October. There she met with a very friendly reception and was celebrated as great statesman (stateswoman) of the world and as a friend of India.

Only a few days later Angela Merkel was in Afghanistan. It was a secret mission. The lightning visit there was treated as state secret for security reasons. Some stages of this first journey of the German chancellor through Afghanistan met the usual what she had on tours through foreign countries. So, for example, the easy press conference on Saturday in the noon under old trees of the garden of the palace of the president of Afghanistan, Hamid Karzai, or that friendly welcome of pupils by the German song "Kommt ein Vogel geflogen" (A Bird Comes A-Flying).

The attendant circumstances of this surprise visit of 24 hours were anything but usual. The lightning visit came near an unreal staging because of the fear of assassinations of Islamic terrorists, which had the security authority of Germany, Afghanistan and other countries. So that was a short stay of Angela Merkel in a country, which was already at war.

In the military base of the German army in Afghanistan, Mazar-e Sharif, Angela Merkel had a talk with coffee and cake together with the soldiers. Whilst she was having coffee break with the soldiers, was arrested a man on the airport of Kabul. He wanted to kill Angela Merkel allegedly. Security officers of Afghanistan meant: "It's good thing that the German chancellor had made use of a helicopter in Kabul and hadn't used a car there"

Merkel's journey to Afghanistan was handled like a state secret up to the landing in Kabul. That happened to reduce the time of preparation for a possible attempt on Merkel's life. In Germany ten persons knew about the planned journey only; the aeroplane was only ordered short time before beginning of the journey. The group for the journey was kept small. The most of the group were bodyguards of the "Bundeskriminalamt" (Detective Office of the German state).

After the landing in Kabul, Angela Markel flew by a military helicopter into the centre of Kabul. The chancellor wore a protecting waistcoat (vest), which could at least absorb small projectiles. She should pass no metre more than essential on the insecure roads of Afghanistan. Also in the air was Merkel protected additionally. Two helicopter gunships of the US-army, model Apache, protected her flight.

On 13 November the popular politician of the SPD, Franz Müntefering, announced his resignation from all political posts. The reason was the illness of his wife. The announcement of the resignation was a political bombshell: Franz Müntefering, also called Münte by his fans, was a social-democratic emphasis in the "grand coalition". He was vice-chancellor and minister for labour. Müntefering wanted to take immediate care of his wife, who had cancer.

In November Angela Markel was travelling again. This time she visited George W. Bush, the President of the United States. Angela Merkel met with a friendly reception at the ranch of Bush. It was a private visit. The American president thought highly of her as important statesman (stateswoman), as important partner in the world and as a friend of the U.S.A. He went by his private car with her through the ranch. During the talks they demonstrated political harmony, with the exception of the protection of climate. Here they had different opinions.

On 20 December were removed the frontier barriers between Germany, Poland and the Czech Republic. By it were also removed the last frontier barriers within the European Union, with the exception the barriers within the European Union with Great Britain, Ireland, Romania, Bulgaria and Cyprus. Just before Christmas, Angela Merkel and the prime ministers of Poland and the Czech Republic had a meeting at the frontier between Poland and Germany. The reason was the ceremony of the great event "Europe without frontiers".

Chronology

1946 Germany, a country of four occupation zones;

Two German regions in the east were

administrated by Poland and the Soviet Union;

A new German Country is born.

1947 The horrible hunger winter;

The German currency RM without value;

A new party in the east of Germany, the SED

The Truman-Doctrine;

The first signs of two German states

1948 A new German National Bank;

The DM is born;

The last German prisoners-of-war were released

by Great Britain;

Talks with the Soviet dictator Stalin;

Trizonesia;

The blockade against West Berlin

1949 Two German constitutions;

The sentence of the last criminals of the Nazi-

regime;

The correction of the German western border;

The first election of the West German state;

Adenauer, the first chancellor of West Germany;

Heuss, the first president of West Germany;

Agreement of Petersberg;

The foundation of the European Council

1950   The foundation of the Montan Union, the first

step on the way to the European Union;

The idea of rearmament of (West) Germany;

The GDR recognized the Oder-Neisse-Line as

Germany's eastern border;

The GDR member of the Comecon;

1951   The French refusal of a (new) German army;

The start of negotiations about a European

Defensive Community;

Baden-Württemberg is born

1952   The "Deutschlandvertrag";

The peace offer of the Soviet Union

1953   Stalin, the dictator of the Soviet Union, dies;

)

Adenauer's journey to the United States;

Election in West Germany, CDU is winner;

1954 The end of the war in Indochina;

Germany, member of the NATO;

The first French-German agreement on Saarland;

The Miracle of Bern

1955 The Treaty of Warsaw;

Austria an independent and neutral state;

The Hallstein-Doctrine;

The people of Saarland want to be Germans;

The release of the last German prisoners of war in

the Soviet Union

1956 The army of the GDR, the *Nationale Volksarmee*;

The Communist Party is declared illegal by the

German Constitutional Court;

Adenauer in Belgium;

Revolution in Hungary

1957 Saarland belongs to (West) Germany;

The "Treaties of Rome", the birth of the European

Union;

The great election victory of Adenauer;

The movement "Battle against the nuclear death";

1958   The East Marches;

The Vice-Minister of the Soviet Union in Bonn;

West Berlin a problem for the Soviet Union;

Heuss, the West German President, in Great Britain;

1959   The treaty about the "European Economic Community " comes into force;

"Schloss Bellevue" in West Berlin seat of the President of West Germany;

Heinrich Lübke, new President of West Germany;

Dwight D. Eisenhower in West Germany;

The foundation of the EEC

1960   The collectivizing of the GDR-agriculture;

The "Production Cooperative of the Manual Workers" in the German Democratic Republic (GDR);

Adenauer travels into the United States and to Japan;

The regulation of the frontier between Germany and the Netherlands;

The people of East Germany were prohibited from using the word "Deutschland" (Germany);

Wilhelm Pieck dies and Walter Ulbricht becomes "Chairman of the Council of State" in East Germany

1961 The Berlin Wall;

Adenauer in the United States again;

1962 The catastrophe of Hamburg

1963 Cuba recognizes the GDR;

Nikita Khrushchev in East Berlin;

The good-will agreement between France and West Germany;

John F. Kennedy in West Berlin, "Ich bin ein Berliner";

Resignation of Adenauer;

John F. Kennedy is killed in Dallas (Texas)

1964 The "mutual assistance and friendship pact"
between the GDR and the Soviet Union;
57 persons escape through self-dug tunnels to
West Berlin

1965 Ludwig Erhard, the new German chancellor, visits
the French President, Charles de Gaulle;
The CDU winner of the election in West Germany

1966 The NPD, neo-Nazi Party, in the Parliament of
Hessen;
Willy Brandt, Foreign Minister of West Germany;
The "APO" appears on the political scene;

1967 Schiller, West German minister for economic
affairs,
Strauß, minister of finance;
The "Konzertierte Aktion";
The Iranian Shah in West Germany;
A student is shot dead during a demonstration;
Adenauer dies;
The beginning of the diplomatic relations with

Romania

1968 Rudi Dutschke, speaker of a protest movement, is
      seriously injured by several shots;
      Attack on the building of the publisher "Axel
      Springer";
      Rebellion in Czechoslovakia;

1969 Gustav Heinemann, new President of West
      Germany;
      Willy Brandt, new Chancellor of West Germany

1970 For the first time a member of the Communist
      government of Poland visits West Germany;
      Terror in Munich;
      Willy Brandt visits the GDR;
      The German ambassador in Guatemala is kid-
      napped;
      The RAF, a new terror group in West Germany;
      Willy Brandt starts with political activities for the
      eastern states;
      West Germany respects the eastern frontiers;
      Willy Brandt in Warsaw

1971 Several diplomatic relations with East European states;

The "Vier-Mächte-Abkommen" of Berlin;

Willy Brandt received the Peace Nobel Prize;

In East Germany Walter Ulbricht is relieved of his duties as "First Secretary"

1972 Problems by the "East Treaties";

The "Verkehrsvertrag" of West Germany with East Germany;

The "Grundvertrag" of West Germany with East Germany;

Terror attack in Brühl, a little town close to Cologne;

Palestinian terrorists kill members of the Israelite Olympic team in Bavaria;

The Euro is called as European Currency

1973 Denmark, Ireland and Great Britain become members of the European Community;

The Secretary General of the Communist Party of the Soviet Union visits the West German capital;

Walter Ulbricht dies;

50,000 Germans have the possibility to leave

Silesia, East Pomerania and East Prussia;

1974 A West German Department of Environment in

West Berlin;

The "Bundesrat" rejects the German-Czech

"Treaty of Normalization";

Walter Scheel, new President of West Germany;

Members of the terror group "Baader-Meinhof"

on hunger strike;

1975 The end of the hunger strike of the members of

the "Baader-Meinhof" group;

Bomb attack by the RAF;

Members of the terror group RAF are arrested

1976 Spring tide on the North Coast;

Suicide of a member of the RAF;

Bomb attack against HQ of the American Army in

Frankfurt;

Gustav Heinemann, the former President of West

Germany, dies;

1977 Demonstrations against the constructions of
       nuclear power stations;
       The Chief State Prosecutor of West Germany is
       murdered;
       The President of the Employer's Association of
       West Germany is kidnapped and murdered;
       A hijack of a German airplane by Palestinian
       terrorists;
       Suicides of some terrorists of the RAF;

1978 The start for the European Monetary System;
       RAF terrorists are arrested in Dortmund;

1979 Members of the RAF terror group are sentenced;
       Karl Carstens, new President of West Germany;
       A new law that makes possible to sentence Nazi-
       criminals also in future;
       The decision of the NATO to deploy nuclear
       medium-range missiles and other missiles in
       West Germany furthermore

1980 The NPD, the neo-Nazi Party, only an unimportant

splinter party;

The "Wehrsport";

Right-wing extremists murder Vietnamese
refugees;

At the "Oktoberfest" in Munich 12 visitors are
killed by a bomb;

1981   Greece, Portugal and Spain join with the
European Community;

The European Parliament;

The "Sternmarsch" against the NATO;

War right in Poland;

Raising of the minimum amount for West
German visitors in East Germany (DDR/GDR);

Social fear of the West Germans;

This year, the year of the juvenile riots;

The "Instandsetzer" (repairing squatters);

Violent conflicts between police and the
"Movement" in Switzerland;

The meeting of the West German Chancellor
with the Head of Government of East Germany;

1982   Ronald Reagan, the President of the United

States, in Bonn;

A new German party, the Greens, seems to appear;

The new German product, the CD;

The development of the DVD;

1983 The conferences on disarmament of the United States and the Soviet Union;

Rebellion against the putting up of new American and Soviet missiles;

The foundation of the "Green Party";

The (new) movements in West Germany;

1984 The Kießling Affair;

The "Party Donation Lawsuit";

Eutelsat

1985 The attempt on the life of the chairman of MTU and BDLI by the RAF;

The inauguration of the opera house in Dresden, the famous "Semper Oper";

The American President, Ronald Reagan, and the German Chancellor, Helmut Kohl, in Bergen-

Belsen and Bitburg;

The famous speech of the West Ger. President;

Klaus von Klitzing, Nobel Prize winner

1986 The interview with the "Head of State and Party"
of East Germany;
A new bomb attack by the RAF;

1987 Gorbachev, head of the government of the Soviet
Union, confirms his reform line;
Willy Brandt announces his resignation as head of
the SPD;
Hans-Jochen Vogel new leader of the SPD;
Erich Honecker, the head of East Germany, in
West Germany;
The Barschel Affair;
The dead of the border of death (terror wall);

1988 120 persons are arrested by the "Stasi" of East
Germany;
The terrible disaster of Borken;
The catastrophe of Ramstein;
The hostage drama of West Germany

1989 The first West German theatre day in the Soviet
Union;

The political change in Hungary;

The political change in Poland;

The political change in Czechoslovakia;

The resignation of Erich Honecker;

The Monday's Demonstrations of Leipzig;

The 40th anniversary of the GDR;

Egon Krenz, the new political leader in the GDR;

The rally of East Berlin;

The Berlin Wall falls;

The political end of Egon Krenz;

The new strong man in the GDR, Gregor Gysi;

The reform movement of the GDR;

The foundation of a new party in the GDR, the
SPD of East Germany;

The "Round Table";

1990 Mikhail Gorbachev, the head of state of the Soviet
Union, speaks about the reunification of Germany

The conception "Two-Plus-Four";

Germany had to give up its eastern territories

(=25% of the whole of Germany);

The first free election in East Germany, DDR/GDR

The two German states enter into an economic, currency and social welfare union;

The DDR (GDR) also adopts the West German "Kündigungsgesetz";

The parliament of East Germany votes for the reunification;

The "Treaty of Reunification"

Members of the CDU reject to accept the Oder-Neisse Line as German eastern frontier;

The reunification of Germany;

5 new German countries

1991　New states in Europe;

The head of the "Berliner Treuhandanstalt" is killed;

Berlin becomes German capital;

Right-wing violence in Hoyerswerda;

1992　War in Yugoslavia;

New states on the Balkan;

Right-wing violence in Rostock;

Arson attack on town houses of Mölln;

Demonstrations against the intolerance and anti-alien feeling;

The "Fristenlösung", the new law in the whole of Germany;

Erich Honecker in Germany again;

Willy Brandt dies;

This year 438,000 refugees in Germany

1993 The chairman of the SPD announces his retirement;

Arson attack on a Turkish house in Solingen;

Mishaps of the anti-terror troop GSG 9

1994 The year of elections;

Roman Herzog, new President of Germany

1995 Oskar Lafontaine, party leader of the SPD

1996 The beginning of the dismantling of the welfare state;

Berlin and Brandenburg shall be one country, but the people of Brandenburg reject it;

The catastrophe at the airport of Düsseldorf

1997 The natural disaster in East Germany;
The famous "Berlin Speech" of the German
President

1998 The terrible train accident of Germany;
The SPD, the strongest power in parliament;
The Red-Green Coalition;
Gerhard Schröder, Chancellor of Germany;
The election of Mecklenburg-West Pomerania

1999 The civil war of Kosovo;
EURO, the new currency in some countries of
Europe;
Oskar Lafontaine resigns from his post as German
minister of finance;
Johannes Rau, new President of Germany;
The "black accounts";
Günter Grass receives the literary Nobel Prize

2000 The new millennium;
The resignation of the leader of the CDU;

Lothar Bisky, the leader of the new Communist
Party PDS, and Gregor Gysi give up their posts;
The agreement about nuclear power stations;
The petrol price for 1 liter more than 2 DM, which
is still currency for payments;
The Bovine Spongiform Encephalopathy in
Germany;
The prohibition of feeding of animal meal

2001 The resignation of two German ministers;
Hannelore Kohl, wife of the former chancellor,
commits suicide;
The first women in the German army;
The assault on the World Trade Center in New
York

2002 The EURO, the currency for 306 million people in
Europe;
The military offensive against the Taliban in
Afghanistan;
14 Germans die by a terrorist attack in Tunisia;
17 persons are killed by a person running amok in
Erfurt;

The air crash in the south of Germany with more
than 70 dead;
The flood disaster of East Germany

2003   The common meeting of "Bundestag" and French
       National Assembly;
       The "Paris Sause";
       The meeting of "Bundesrat" and French Senate;
       The conference of the French-German youth
       parliament;
       Mounir el Motassadeq, who belongs to the
       terrorist cell of Mohammed Atta, the death pilot
       of New York, is sentenced in Hamburg;
       The great heat in Germany;
       Jürgen W. Möllemann, the former leading
       politician of the Liberal Party, dies as skydiver;
       Gerhard Schröder gives up his post as chairman
       of the SPD;
       Müntefering new leader of the SPD;
       Horst Köhler, new President of Germany;
       In Arromanches (France) is commemorated the
       D-Day;
       The "Hartz IV-Law"

2005 Joseph Cardinal Ratzinger is new pope;

Angela Merkel, new Chancellor of Germany;

2006 Acts of violence at the "Rütli-School" in Berlin;

Ursula von der Leyen, the new minister for family

affairs, presents her "alliance for education";

Montenegro, the new independent state on

Balkan;

2007 The summit conference of the 27 states of the

European Union;

Germany's problem with Poland;

The actions of German expellees against Poland;

The atrocious murders of Duisburg, 6 Italians are

executed;

Germans are killed in Afghanistan;

Islamic terrorists in Germany;

The visit of the Dalai Lama to Germany;

Angela Merkel in South Africa;

Peter Grünberg, a German physicist, winner of

the Nobel Prize;

Gerhard Ertl, another German winner of the

Nobel Prize;

Angela Merkel in India;

Angela Merkel in Afghanistan;

Müntefering resigns from his posts as vice-chancellor and minister for labor;

The ceremony "Europe without frontiers"

Important persons

ABBA, Swedish pop group (1972 – 1982)

Ackermann, Anton, Communist leader of the GDR
(1905 – 1973)

Adenauer, Konrad, German Chancellor 1949 – 1963
(1876 – 1967)

Albrecht, Susanne, RAF-terrorist (1951 -- ….)

al-Motassadeq, Mounir, Moroccan terrorist (1974 -- ….)

Baader, Andreas, RAF-terrorist (1943 – 1977)

Bahr, Egon, Permanent Secretary of the Chancellery of
West Germany (1922 – 2015)

Baker, James, Secretary of State of the United States
(1930 -- ….)

Barschel, Uwe, Minister President of Schleswig-Holstein
(1944 – 1987)

Barzel, Rainer, party leader of the CDU (1924 – 2006)

Baudouin I, King of Belgium (1930 – 1993)

Beck, Kurt, Minister President of Rhineland-Palatinate
(1949 -- ….)

Beckurts, Karl Heinz, manager of the company Siemens
(1930 – 1986)

Benedict XVI, pope, see also Ratzinger (1927 -- ….)

Ben-Gurion, David, Israeli Prime Minister (1886 – 1973)

Berberich, Monika, RAF-terrorist (1942 -- ….)

Beuys, Joseph, professor at the Academy of Art in
Düsseldorf (1921 – 1986)

Bevin, Ernest, British Foreign Secretary (1881 – 1951)

bin Laden, Osama, head of the terror organization Al-
Qaida (1957 – 2011)

Bisky, Lothar, leader of a new German party, PDS
(1941 – 2013)

Bohley, Bärbel, founder of a new political movement in
East Germany (1945 – 2010)

Böhmer, Wolfgang, Minister President of Saxony-Anhalt
(1936 -- ….)

Böll, Heinrich, German author (1917 – 1985)

Bouffier, Volker, Hessian minister of the interior
(1951 -- ….)

Brandt, Willy, Mayor of West Berlin, then German
Chancellor (1913 – 1992)

Breuel, Birgit, head of the Berlin Trust Agency-Treu-
handanstalt (1937 -- ….)

Brezhnev, Leonid, leader of the Soviet Union
(1906 – 1982)

Britting, Georg, German lyric poet (1891 – 1964)

Buback, Siegfried, West German Chief State Prosecutor
(1920 – 1977)

Bulganin, Nikolai, Prime Minister of the Soviet Union
(1895 – 1975)

Burakiewicz, Janusz, Polish Foreign Minister
(1916 – 1989)

Bush, George Walker, American President (1946 -- ....)

Byrnes, James, American Secretary of State and General
Marshal (1879 – 1972)

Carl XVI Gustaf, King of Sweden (1946 -- ....)

Carlson, Per, head of the Nobel Committee (? -- ....)

Carstens, Karl, West German President (1914 – 1992)

Černik, Oldřich, Prime Minister of Czechoslovakia
(1921 – 1994)

Charles de Gaulle, French President 1958 – 1969
(1890 – 1970)

Chirac, Jacques, President of France (1932 -- ....)

Churchill, Winston, Prime Minister of the United King-
dom 1940 – 1945 and 1951 – 1955 (1874 – 1965)

Císař, Čestmir, chairman of the "Central Committee of
Czechoslovakia" (1920 – 2013)

Connally, John, Governor of Texas (1917 – 1993)

Connally, Nellie, wife of John Connally (1919 – 2006)

Dalai Lama, Tenzin Gyatso, Holy Tibetan Buddhist monk
(1935 -- ....)

de Maizière, Lothar, Prime Minister of East Germany-
GDR (1940 -- ....)

Degowski, Dieter, German bank robber (? -- ....)

Dehler, Thomas, German politician of the FDP
(1897 – 1967)

Dollmann, Georg von, German architect (1830 – 1895)

Dönitz, Karl, last President of the German Reich
(1891 – 1980)

Dubček, Alexander, leader of the Czech Communist
Party (1921 – 1992)

Dulles, John Foster, US Secretary of State (1888 – 1959)

Dumas, Roland, Foreign Minister of France (1922 -- ....)

Dutschke Rudi, speaker of a protest movement
(1940 – 1979)

Ebert, Friedrich, German Chancellor of the Weimar
Republic (1871 – 1925)

Ebert, Friedrich, member of the SED (1894 – 1979)

Eden, Anthony, Prime Minister, UK (1897 – 1977)

Ehard, Hans, Minister President of Bavaria (1887 – 1980)

Eichel, Hans, German Minister of Finance (1941 -- ....)

Eisenhower, Dwight D., American President

(1890 – 1969)

Elisabeth II, Queen of 16 Commonwealth Nations
(1926 -- ….)

Engholm, Björn, SPD leader in Schleswig-Holstein
(1939 -- ….)

Ensslin, Gudrun, RAF-terrorist (1940 – 1977)

Eppelmann, Rainer, Protestant pastor in East Germany
(1943 -- ….)

Erhard, Ludwig, German Chancellor (1897 – 1977)

Ertl, Gerhard, German chemist (1936 -- ….)

Fert, Albert, French physicist (1938 -- ….)

Fischer, Andrea, German Minister of Health (1960 -- ….)

Fischer, Joschka, German Foreign Minister (1948 -- ….)

Flick, Friedrich Karl, German industrialist (1927 – 2006)

Fotyga, Anna, Polish Foreign Minister (1957 -- …)

Frahm, Herbert Ernst Karl, this was the former name
of Willy Brandt

Frick, Wilhelm, NS-Minister for Interior (1877 – 1946)

Friedrichs, Hans, German Economy Minister (1931 -- ….)

Frings, Joseph, Cardinal and Archbishop of Cologne
(1887 – 1978)

Fritsche, Hans, Journalist and speaker of the German
Broadcasting (1900 – 1953)

Funk, Walter, German Minister for Economic Affairs

(1890 – 1960)

Funke, Karl-Heinz, German Minister for Agriculture

(1946 -- ….)

Galinski, Heinz, chairman of the Jewish Community of

West Berlin (1912 – 1992)

Genscher, Hans-Dietrich, German Foreign Minister

(1927 – 2016)

Gierek, Edward, leader of the Polish Communist Party

(1913 – 2001)

Globke, Hans, Consultant of Adenauer (1898 – 1973)

Göbel, Wolfgang, driver of Siegfried Buback (? – 1977)

Goebbels, Joseph, Reich Minister of Propaganda

(1897 – 1945)

Gorbachev, Mikhail, head of government of the Soviet

Union (1931 -- ….)

Göring, Hermann, Supreme Commander of the German

Air Force (1893 – 1946)

Grass, Günter, German author (1927 – 2015)

Gromyko, Andrej, Soviet Foreign Minister (1909 – 1989)

Groppler, Eckhard, driver of Karl Heinz Beckurts

(? – 1986)

Grotewohl, Otto, Prime Minister of East Germany

(1894 – 1964)

Grünberg, Peter, German physicist (1939 -- ….)

Guillaume, Christel, wife of Günter Guillaume and spy of

East Germany (1927 – 2004)

Guillaume, Günter, personal assistant of Willy Brand, spy

of East Germany (1927 – 1995)

Gysi, Gregor, head of a new German party, PDS

(1948 -- ….)

Hahn, Otto, German chemist (1879 – 1968)

Haley, Bill, American "Rock – 'n' – Roll" musician

(1925 – 1981)

Hallstein, Walter, German journalist, teacher and

politician (1901 – 1982)

Hammarskjöld, Dag, Secretary-General of the UNO

(1905 – 1961)

Hartz, Peter, German industry manager (1941 -- ….)

Hein, Christoph, author and representative of the East

German opposition (1944 -- ….)

Heinemann, Gustav, West German President

(1899 – 1976)

Heinrich II, German emperor (973 – 1024)

Heisenberg, Werner, German physicist (1901 – 1976)

Herzog, Roman, German President (1934 -- ….)

Heß, Rudolf, Hitler's substitute (1894 – 1987)

Heuss, Theodor, first president of West Germany

(1884 – 1963)

Heym, Stefan, author and representative of the East German opposition (1913 – 2001)

Himmler, Heinrich, Reichsführer SS (1900 – 1945)

Hitler, Adolf, German dictator (1889 – 1945)

Hochhuth, Rolf, German author (1931 -- ….)

Hoffmann, Karl-Heinz, founder of a right-wing military

sports club (1937 -- ….)

Holzmann Philipp, today a known construction company

Holzmann, (Johann) Philipp, he was manufacturer of

railroad tracks (1805 – 1870)

Honecker, Erich, Communist leader of government in

East Germany (1912 – 1994)

Horn, Gyula, Hungarian Foreign Minister (1932 – 2013)

Hupka, Herbert, at first member of the SPD, then CDU

(1915 – 2006)

Hurd, Douglas, Foreign Secretary of Great Britain

(1930 -- ….)

Immendorff, Jörg, professor at the Academy of Art in

Düsseldorf (1945 – 2007)

Jenninger, Philipp, President of the German Bundestag

1984 - 1988 (1932 -- ....)

John Paul II, pope (1920 – 2005)

Johnson, Lyndon B., US Vice-President, then President of
the United States (1908 – 1973)

Johnson, Uwe, German author (1934 – 1984)

Kaczyński, Jaroslaw Aleksander, Prime Minister of
Poland 2006-2007 (1949 -- ....)

Kaczyński, Lech Aleksander, brother of Jaroslaw Aleksander, Polish President 2005-2010 (1949 – 2010)

Kaiser, Jakob, CDU politician (1888 – 1961)

Karzai, Hamid, President of Afghanistan (1957 -- ....)

Keitel, Wilhelm, German Field Marshal (1882 – 1946)

Kennan, George, American State Department
(1904 – 2005)

Kennedy, Jacqueline, wife of John F. Kennedy
(1929 – 1994)

Kennedy, John F., American President 1961 – 1963
(1917 – 1963)

Keynes, John Maynard, English economist (1883 – 1946)

Khrushchev, Nikita, leader of the Soviet Union 1958 –
1964 (1894 – 1971)

Kiesinger, Kurt Georg, Chancellor of West Germany 1966
– 1969 (1904 – 1988)

Kießling, Günter, German "four-star general"

(1925 – 2009)

Kipphardt, Heinar, German author (1922 – 1982)

Kohl, Hannelore, wife of Helmut Kohl (1933 – 2001)

Kohl, Helmut, German Chancellor 1982 – 1998

(1930 – 2017)

Kohl, Michael, Cabinet Council of GDR/East Germany

(1929 – 1981)

Köhler, Gundolf, neo-Nazi (1959 – 1980)

Köhler, Horst, Germ. President 2004 – 2010 (1943 -- ….)

Kosygin, Aleksey Nikolayevich, Soviet Prime Minister

1964 – 1980 (1904 – 1980)

Krause, Günter, parliamentary permanent secretary in

East Germany (1953 -- ….)

Krenz, Egon, Secretary of the East German party SED in

1989 (1937 -- ….)

Künast, Renate, German Min. for Consumer Protection,

Feeding and Agriculture 2001 – 2005 (1955 -- ….)

Lafontaine, Oskar, German Minister of Finance

(1943 – …)

Lambsdorff, Otto Graf, German politician of the Liberal

Party (1926 – 2009)

Lemmer, Ernst, CDU politician in East Germany

(1898 – 1970)

Leonhard, Wolfgang, historian and Communist of East
Germany (1921 – 2014)

Ley, Robert, Reichsarbeiterführer (1890 – 1945)

Liebknecht, Karl, German Communist leader
(1871 – 1919)

Lorenz, Peter, chairman of the CDU in West Berlin
(1922 – 1987)

Lübke, Heinrich, West German President (1894 – 1972)

Luxemburg, Rosa, German Communist leader
(1871 – 1919)

Mahler, Horst, RAF-terrorist (1936 -- ….)

Major, John, Prime Minister of Great Britain (1943 -- ….)

Mandela, Nelson, President of South Africa (1918 – 2013

Marshall, George Catlett, American Secretary of State
(1880 – 1959)

Mataré, Ewald, German sculptor (1887 – 1965)

Mathiopoulos, Margarita, press spokeswoman of the
SPD (1956 -- ….)

Mazowiecki, Tadeusz, head of the Polish government
(1927 – 2013)

McCloy, John Jay, American High Commissioner in West
Germany (1895 – 1989)

Meinhof, Ulrike, RAF-terrorist (1934 – 1976)

Meins, Holger Klaus, RAF-terrorist (1941 – 1974)

Mende, Erich, Chairman of the FDP (1916 – 1998)

Merkel, Angela Dorothea, head of the party CDU and
German Chancellor (1954 -- ….)

Mikoyan, Anastas, Soviet Vice-Prime Minister
(1895 – 1978)

Mitterrand, François, French President (1916 – 1996)

Modrow, Hans, Prime Minister of East Germany/GDR
(1928 -- ….)

Möllemann, Jürgen W., leader of the party FDP
(1945 – 2003)

Molotov, Vyacheslav Mikhaylovich, Russian Foreign
Minister (1890 – 1986)

Momper, Walter, Mayor of West Berlin (1945 -- ….)

Müller, Hermann, German chancellor of the "Weimar
Republic" (1876 – 1931)

Müller, Werner, German Minister for Economic Affairs
(1946 -- ….)

Müntefering, Franz, chairman of the SPD and German
Transport Minister (1940 -- ….)

Niser bin Muhammad Nasar Nawar, Tunisian terrorist
(1978 – 2002)

Novotný, Antonin, President of Czechoslovakia (

(1904 – 1975)

Oettinger, Günther, Minister President of Baden-

Württemberg (1953 -- ....)

Ohm, Georg Simon, German physicist (1789 – 1854)

Ohnesorg, Benno, German student (1940 – 1967)

Ollenhauer, Erich, chairman of the SPD (1901 – 1963)

Olszowski, Stefan, Polish Foreign Minister (1931 -- ....)

Orff, Carl, German composer (1895 – 1982)

Oswald, Lee Harvey, likely murderer of John F. Kennedy

(1939 – 1963)

Otto, Teo, German painter (1904 – 1968)

Oxfort, Hermann, member of the FDP (1928 – 2003)

Pfeiffer, Reiner, senior official in the State Office of Kiel

(1939 -- ....)

Pieck, Wilhelm, Communist politician in East Germany

(1876 – 1960)

Plambeck, Juliane, RAF-terrorist (1952 – 1980)

Platzeck, Matthias, leader of the SPD and Minister

President of Brandenburg (1953 -- ....)

Plenzdorf, Ulrich, German author (1934 – 2007)

Pleven, René, French Prime Minister (1901 – 1993)

Ponto, Jürgen, speaker of the Dresdner Bank

(1923 – 1977)

Quidde, Ludwig, German historian and liberal politician
(1858 – 1941)

Raeder, Erich, Commander-in-chief of the German navy
(1876 – 1960)

Raspe, Jan-Carl, RAF-terrorist (1944 – 1977)

Ratzinger, Joseph Aloisius, he was Cardinal and became
pope under the name Benedict XVI

Rau, Johannes, Minister President of North Rhine-Westphalia, German President (1931 – 2006)

Reagan, Ronald, American President (1911 – 2004)

Reich, Jens, founder of a new political movement in East
Germany (1939 -- ….)

Reinders, Ralf, RAF-terrorist (1948 -- ….)

Reuter, Ernst, Mayor of West Berlin (1889 – 1953)

Reza Pahlavi, Iranian Shah (1919 – 1980)

Ringstorff, Harald, Minister President of Mecklenburg-
West Pomerania (1939 -- ….)

Rohwedder, Detlev Karsten, head of the
"Treuhandanstalt"/Trust Agency (1932 – 1991)

Rollnik, Gebriele, RAF-terrorist, today author!
(1950 -- ….)

Röntgen, Wilhelm Conrad, German physicist

(1845 – 1923)

Rösner, Hans-Jürgen, German bank robber (? -- ….)

Ruby, Jack, owner of an American night club

(1911 – 1967)

Runge, Erika, German author (1939 -- ….)

Rütli-School, grammar school in Berlin, named after an
important historical Swiss place

Schabowski, Günter, head of the party SED in East Berlin

(1929 -- ….)

Schacht, Hjalmar, President of the German National
Bank (1877 – 1970)

Scharping, Rudolf, German Minister of Defense and SPD
party leader (1947 -- ….)

Schäuble, Wolfgang, German Minister of the Interior,
later of "finance" (1942 -- ….)

Scheel, Walter, German Foreign Minister, President of
West Germany (1919 -- ….)

Schickele, René, French-German writer (1883 – 1940)

Schiller, Friedrich, famous German writer (1759 – 1805)

Schiller, Karl, German Minister of Finance (1911 – 1994)

Schleyer, Hanns-Martin, German manager (1915 – 1977)

Schmidt, Helmut, Chancellor of West Germany

(1918 -- ….)

Schmidt, Ulla, German Minister for Health (1949 -- ....)

Schorlemmer, Friedrich, pastor and man of the East
German opposition (1944 -- ....)

Schröder, Gerhard 1), CDU, minister posts: Interior,
Foreign, Defense (1910 – 1989)

Schröder, Gerhard 2), SPD, chancellor of Germany
in the years 1998 – 2005 (1944 -- ....)

Schumacher, Kurt, leader of the SPD (1895 – 1952)

Schuman, Robert, French Prime Minister (1886 – 1963)

Sciasca, Lorenzo, Swiss architect (1643 - 1694)

Seyß-Inquart, Arthur, "Reichskommissar" for the
Netherlands (1892 – 1946)

Shevardnadze, Eduard, Foreign Minister of the Soviet
Union (1928 – 2014)

Skubiszewski, Krzysztof, Polish Foreign Minister
(1926 – 2010)

Smirnov, Andrey Andreyevich, Soviet ambassador in
West Germany (1905 – 1982)

Smrkovský, Josef, President of the Czechoslovakian
National Assembly (1911 – 1974)

Sobottka, Gustav, German politician (1886 – 1953)

Sokolovsky, Vasili Danilovich, Soviet military governor in
East Germany (1897 – 1968)

Speer, Albert, NS-War Minister (1905 – 1981)

Spira, Steffi, actor and representative of the East

German opposition (1908 – 1995)

Springer, Axel, publisher of newspapers (1912 – 1985)

Stoiber, Edmund, leader of the party CSU and Minister

President of Bavaria (1941 -- ....)

Stollmann, Jost, a German businessman (1955 -- ....)

Stoph, Willi, Vice-Prime Minister in East Germany/GDR

(1914 – 1999)

Strauß, Franz Josef, Bavarian Minister President

(1915 – 1988)

Streicher, Julius, Gau-leader of Franconia (1885 – 1946)

Stresemann, Gustav, German Chancellor, later Foreign

Minister (1878 – 1929)

Struck, Karin, German author (1947 – 2006)

Stücklen, Richard, member of the Bavarian Christian

Party (1916 – 2002)

Svoboda, Ludvik, President of Czechoslovakia

(1895 – 1979)

Teufel, Fritz, member of the German protest movement

of students (1943 – 2010)

Tiedge, Hansjoachim, West German Protector of

Constitution and Russian spy (1937 – 2011)

Trittin, Jürgen, Germ. Minister of Environment (1954- ...)

Truman, Harry S., American President (1884 – 1972)

Ulbricht, Walter, Head of Government in East
Germany/GDR (1893 – 1973)

Viett, Inge, RAF-terrorist, today author! (1944 -- ....)

Vogel, Hans-Jochen, party leader of the SPD (1926 -- ....)

von Baudissin, Wolf Graf, German general (1907 – 1993)

von Brauchitsch, Eberhard, German manager
(1926 – 2010)

von Braunmühl, Gerold, German diplomat (1935 – 1986)

von der Leyen, Ursula, German Minister for Family
Affairs (1958 -- ....)

von Drenkmann, Günter, President of the Chamber
Court West Berlin (1910 – 1974)

von Klitzing, Klaus, German physicist (1943 -- ....)

von Ossietzky, Carl, German journalist and author
(1889 – 1938)

von Papen, Franz, the so-called "Holder of Hitler's
stirrup" (1879 – 1969)

von Ribbentrop, Joachim, German Minister for
Economic Affairs (1890 – 1960)

von Spreti, Karl Marie Graf, German ambassador in
Guatemala (1907 – 1970)

von Weizsäcker, Carl Friedrich, West German President
   1984 – 1990, then till 1994 Germ. Pres. (1920 – 2015)

Wallraff, Günter, German author (1942 -- ….)

Warren, Christopher, American Secretary of State
   (1925 – 2011)

Wehner, Herbert, vice-chairman of the SPD (1906 – 1990

Weiss, Peter, German author (1916 – 1982)

Westerwelle, Guido, German Foreign Minister
   (1961 –2016)

Wolf, Christa, author and representative of the East
   German opposition (1929 – 2011)

Wolf, Christa, German author (1929 – 2011)

Wolf, Markus, head of the secret service of East
   Germany (1923 – 2006)

Wörner, Manfred, German Minister of Defense, NATO
   Secretary General (1934 – 1994)

Wulff, Christian, Minister President of Lower Saxony,
   then German President (1959 -- ….)

Yeltsin, Boris Nikolayevich, President of Russia
   (1931 – 2007)

Zhdanov, Andrei, Soviet politician (1896 – 1948)

Zimmermann, Ernst, high German industry manager
   (1929 – 1985)

Bibliography

Deutsche Geschichte, Band 12; Heinrich Pleticha, 1984

Die Große Bertelsmann Lexikothek, Band 1 – 15, 1988

Die Chronik, Geschichte des 20. Jahrhunderts bis heute,

2006

Wikipedia

Various German newspapers and German TV also served as sources of information.

Note

Due to lack of imaging permissions, no strange photos were taken that are less than 70 years old. Thus these photos are no longer protected under copyright because their first release dates back more than 50 years. The drawings were made by myself. The other pictures are copies of my own photos.

The author

Books about German history by Egon Harings

German(ic) History Volume 1 *The great time of the Germanic tribes*	published by August von Goethe Literaturverlag/ Frankfurt in 2010 and Fouqué Publishers/New York in 2012
German History Volume 2 *Germany in the Middle Ages*	published by August von Goethe Literaturverlag/ Frankfurt in 2011
Germany before and after the Thirty-Years' War *From Martin Luther to the French Revolution*	not published yet
Germany before World War I *From Napoleon to the signs of World War I*	not published yet

Germany and two World Wars   not published yet

From the German Reich to the

end of the Nazi regime

Germany after World War II

Two German states and their

* reunification*

The Great Age of Angela Merkel   published by

tredition in 2017

The last years of the reign of   publication

Angela Merkel   planned

Zeitfracht Medien GmbH
Ferdinand-Jühlke-Straße 7
99095 Erfurt, Deutschland
produktsicherheit@kolibri360.de